T0066693

War and Religion: A Very Short Introduction

VERY SHORT INTRODUCTIONS are for anyone wanting a stimulating and accessible way into a new subject. They are written by experts, and have been translated into more than 45 different languages.

The series began in 1995, and now covers a wide variety of topics in every discipline. The VSI library currently contains over 650 volumes—a Very Short Introduction to everything from Psychology and Philosophy of Science to American History and Relativity—and continues to grow in every subject area.

Very Short Introductions available now:

For more information visit our website

www.oup.com/vsi/

Jolyon Mitchell and Joshua Rey

WAR AND RELIGION

A Very Short Introduction

OXFORD

UNIVERSITY PRESS

OXFORD

UNIVERSITY PRESS

Great Clarendon Street, Oxford, OX2 6DP,
United Kingdom

Oxford University Press is a department of the University of Oxford.
It furthers the University's objective of excellence in research, scholarship,
and education by publishing worldwide. Oxford is a registered trade mark of
Oxford University Press in the UK and in certain other countries

© Jolyon Mitchell and Joshua Rey 2021

The moral rights of the authors have been asserted

First edition published in 2021

Impression: 1

Published in the United States of America by Oxford University Press
198 Madison Avenue, New York, NY 10016, United States of America

British Library Cataloguing in Publication Data
Data available

Library of Congress Control Number: 2020946915

ISBN 978-0-19-880321-8

Printed in Great Britain by
Ashford Colour Press Ltd, Gosport, Hampshire

Contents

Acknowledgements

This is a very short introduction to a huge topic, which builds on the rich and insightful work of many scholars who have worked on different aspects of the relation between religion and war. The annotated and selective bibliography is a token of our thanks to some of those who have already explored this area. Their work, among others, has been invaluable to our own, teaching us how much there is still to learn and to understand in this complex and often contested field. We are indebted to the anonymous readers for their helpful comments and to Naomi Appleton, Anna King, Kevin Reinhardt, Joshua Ralston, and Jolyon Thomas for their careful reading and useful observations on various aspects of earlier draft chapters. We are also grateful to many others including Nick Adams, Scott Appleby, Catharine Beck, Nigel Biggar, Iona Birchall, Helen Bond, Kit and Janet Bowen, David Clough, Stephen Edmonds, David Craig, Tim Dean, David Fergusson, David Ford, Jamie and Sandy Frost, Theodora Hawksley, Stewart Hoover, Tim Jenkins, John Paul Lederach, Allan Little, Alan and Kate Mclean, Alex and Nadine Matheson, Hannah Holtschneider, Suzanna Millar, Peter Mitchell, Ebrahim Moosa, David Morgan, Michael Northcott, Oliver O'Donovan, Atalia Omer, Charles Pickstone, Shadaab Rahemtulla, David Rosen, Bettina Schmidt, Ulrich Schmiedel, Mona Siddiqui, David Smith, Brian Stanley, Geoffrey and Judith Stevenson, Steve Sutcliffe, Sarah Synder, Susie Synder, Michael Wakelin, Charles and Sarah Warren, Jo and Sam Wells,

Deborah Whitehead, George Wilkes, Mike Wooldridge, for their many encouragements, insightful remarks, hospitality and swift answers to questions. Thanks also to Andrea Keegan and Jenny Nugee at OUP for their wise editorial advice and careful attention to detail, as well as the entire production team (including Sandy Garel and Emma Varley at OUP; Ethiraju Saraswathi and Nivedha Vinayagamurthy at SPi Global).

Jolyon Mitchell is grateful to his colleagues at the BBC World Service who first taught him about some of the difficulties of covering and explaining the relation between war and religion in different parts of the world. He is also thankful to all his colleagues and students at New College, CTPI, IASH, and other parts of the University of Edinburgh, as well as other scholars of religion from around the UK and beyond, for further illuminating his understanding of the topic. To his family, Clare, Jasmine, Xanthe, and Sebastian, a huge thank you.

Joshua Rey is grateful to the good friends who challenged his unexamined atheism in the early 1990s; and to those with whom, partly as a result, he later found himself working in Afghanistan, both colleagues and members of the Taliban administration, for many good conversations on comparative religion; for the stimulating experience of working in the religious diversity of Eastern Sri Lanka; and to all those from whom he learned, and with whom he has lived, Christian theology, as an ordinand and a clergyman in the Church of England. Above all he is grateful to Annie, *sine qua non*.

Both authors are grateful to each other for instructive, robust, and collegial disagreement about many of the topics in this book.

List of illustrations

Chapter 1
Remembering wars

In a grainy video, a sea of young Iranian men surges into an army depot to begin their service as soldiers in the Iran–Iraq war (1980–8). As they march and assemble, a singer rhythmically declaims the names of those who have already given their lives in the fighting. The soldiers, now in fatigues, clap along, or slap their heads with both hands in time to the pulsating music. Men are being bonded by song, rhythm, ritual, and shared emotion, to prepare for what is to come. At the end of the film, silhouettes of soldiers are outlined against the setting sun as the song returns again and again to the same refrain: 'Karbala…Karbala…'

Another scene: quieter but no less powerful. White headstones stand in rows and columns arranged across clipped green turf. Each bears a name, rank, unit, date, and age, and perhaps a more personal dedication composed by relatives. You can see this scene in cemeteries across the world where soldiers of the former British Empire are buried. The focal point is usually a simple white stone cross on which is mounted a bronze sword: 'The Cross of Sacrifice'.

Take one more image: an artefact in the Smithsonian Institution in Washington DC. A white shirt with long purple fringes at wrists and waist, bunches of feathers hanging from the shoulders, an eagle embroidered on the back. In the 1880s this and similar garments were worn by men of the Lakota and other Great Plains communities as they moved together in a prolonged mesmeric circle: the Ghost Dance.

A song about a city built on a battlefield, sung by men preparing for war. A cross with a sword on it—or a sword on a cruciform stone. A shirt trusted to ward off bullets, now in the national museum of the country that sent the rifles. Here are loss, and the longing for hope; sacrifice, death, and something beyond death. Reflecting on these symbols, we can start to build a picture of how war and religion mingle and shape one another.

Karbala martyrs: past, present, and still to come

One of the most important days in the Shi'a Muslim calendar, and certainly a day which, since the Islamic Revolution in Iran, has taken on the highest political significance, is Ashura, the anniversary of the Battle of Karbala, 10 October 680. For half a century after the death of Muhammad, tension grew between those who followed descendants of Ali, Muhammad's cousin, and those who believed Abu Bakr, and the caliphs after him, were the Prophet's successors, a tension which led ultimately to the division between Shi'a and Sunni. A turning point was the Battle of Karbala, in which Husayn ibn Ali and his followers were defeated by a larger force loyal to the Caliph Yazid.

Ever since, the story has been re-enacted in many forms, retelling how the battle lasted ten days, the hero Husayn defeating a string of soldiers in single combat, before succumbing to overwhelming numbers of the opposition. The suffering of Husayn and his followers was extreme; Yazid's cavalry are said to have blockaded the Euphrates, so that Husayn's party had to fight without water. And in the telling and retelling of this story, Husayn and his followers became the founding martyrs of Shi'a Islam. The iconography of thirst and multiple wounds is enshrined in annual commemorations in which devotees inflict similar sufferings on themselves, thereby entering into the martyrdom of Husayn.

These Karbala processions and the later 'passion plays' grew in importance during the Safavid dynasty (1501–1736) and today are followed by huge audiences, physically present and watching on YouTube. Large casts and high production values make them high-profile events in which audiences and cast alike enter with deep emotion, sharing in suffering and confessing guilt for complicity in its infliction.

The Karbala story has had great power in Shi'a Islam down the centuries and its imagery has been used to frame and interpret contemporary events in different ways. A striking example is the Iranian memorialization of the Iran–Iraq war (1980–8). Both countries have a Shi'a majority, but the Iraqi leader, Saddam Hussein, was a secularized Sunni, who had treated Shi'ites in Iraq severely. This made it easy for Iran to frame the war as an echo of the Battle of Karbala.

The Karbala story was already important in the rhetoric of Iran's revolution, in which the Shah had been compared to Yazid; but it was in the 1980s that this imagery was most powerful. Ayatollah Khomeini (1902–89) and other Iranian leaders drew on the imagery of the Karbala story to mobilize the population for war, praying in a 1983 sermon, 'cause us to be among the people of Karbala'. Saddam Hussein was Yazid; Iranian soldiers could have the privilege of becoming Husayn.

As the war progressed and the casualties mounted, the need to give meaning to suffering on the battlefield was often met with the symbolism of the Karbala martyrs, whilst on the home front, media helped forge a narrative to motivate young men to sacrifice. These two agendas were closely intertwined, and worked out in similar forms.

Murals and posters commemorating the war dead appeared across Iran, often drawing parallels between the death of soldiers and the martyrdom of Husayn. In one Tehran mural a young soldier in contemporary military fatigues carries a modern rifle, but around his head is a red band emblazoned with the text 'O, the shining moon of the tribe of Hashim [Husayn]'. Behind him is the golden dome of Husayn's shrine at Karbala, in what is now Iraq. A 1981 poster depicts an Iranian soldier being shot: behind him, holding his white horse, is Imam Husayn (see Figure 1). They are connected by a green cloak which they both hold, implying that Husayn is about to pull him into paradise. On the left are three headless figures, 'fellow martyrs who died with Husayn at the Battle of Karbala'. These and many other images draw on the iconography of the Karbala martyrdoms, the primal example of self-sacrifice, central to the identity of Shi'a Islam.

In this interplay between religion and war, a number of themes come into focus. Religion provides symbolism heavily loaded with accessible meaning and rhetorical force. It can be used both to mobilize societies to fight wars, and also to soften the sense of loss by making death in war part of a noble and significant story.

The concept of a martyr is interesting here. A victory from which combatants return whole and alive tells its own story of purpose and hope; to be bereaved through war with no winners, by contrast, can be heartbreaking and meaningless. In the midst of loss and defeat, the concept of martyrdom may offer, for some, a kind of comfort. The martyr is one who dies a seemingly purposeless death which, in the light of eternity, turns out to have cosmic significance.

For some, seeing those they have lost as martyrs may help give an answer to the question what sense can be made of such terrible deaths. Of course, another possible answer to this question is 'no sense at all'. Some may be reduced to this, and indeed may take comfort from its starkness. When those who sorrow seek to fill the void of meaning that war opens up, however, they often call on the resources of religion.

1. *The Martyr, c.*1981. The poster resonates with Iranian 'Ashura mourning rituals, which encourage soldiers to see themselves as following in the path of the Karbala martyrs.'

The Cross of Sacrifice: Great War memorials

The Iran–Iraq conflict, with its trenches, its poison gas, and its flavour of unfathomable stalemate, carries powerful echoes of the First World War (1914–18). This war has come to be a paradigm of purposeless loss. With all the powerful nations of the day engaged, the roll of casualties was immense. The last war fought on the continent of Europe had been a century earlier, and though Waterloo was a catastrophic battle, its death and destruction was on a far smaller scale. It was possible, at least in hindsight, to romanticize the Napoleonic Wars as colourful and chivalric. Not so the Great War.

It began, indeed, in a spirit of often romantic patriotism on all sides. In the early stages there was a place for hope. Rupert Brooke, preparing for battle, as he thought, and addressing those who would remember him should he die, could write in 'The Soldier' of a heart cleansed by death, 'all evil shed away', 'a pulse in the eternal mind' and finally 'at peace, under an English heaven'. But Brooke never fought in the trenches. He died in 1915, only a year after writing this poem, of sepsis, en route to Gallipoli. In the years of fighting that followed, Brooke's beatific vision of noble death proved unsustainable.

For some, religion itself seemed emptied of power. The immense horror of the battle drowned out any attempt to lend dignity to death. In 'Anthem for Doomed Youth' Wilfred Owen plays on the ringing of a 'passing bell' in a country church to call the village to pray when a villager died. This ancient, gentle, communal custom cannot survive the mechanized horror of the Western Front: 'What passing-bells for these who die as cattle? Only the monstrous anger of the guns.'

Wilfred Owen's post-religious despair was widely echoed. Nevertheless, whilst religious ideals were sometimes tested to breaking point by the Great War, the immense void of meaning it opened up demanded to be filled. To meet this need, nations, towns, villages, families, and individuals did in practice draw on religion to a very great extent. Jay Winter articulates this paradoxical quality of remembrance very well in his 1995 cultural history of the Great War, *Sites of Mourning, Sites of Memory*. He argues that this, the most 'modern' of wars, set off an avalanche of the 'unmodern'. As the scientific revolution reached its apotheosis in ever more efficient ways of killing, many turned again to religion seeking a kind of meaning that science could not offer.

Although this sometimes took unusual forms, some turning to spiritualism with its promise of direct communication with the dead, for the most part it was conventional religion that filled this void of meaning. This was distinctively so in England, where Church and State were closely intertwined, and although many other denominations flourished, the Established Church was at the centre of most acts of remembrance. Great War memorials started to go up early in the war. To begin with they were commonly 'rolls of honour' listing those who had volunteered to fight. Often improvised local roadside shrines, they spread rapidly from 1916 onwards. As the war continued, however, the focus moved from the living to the dead. Communities began to feel the need for more formal memorials. Local government, newspapers, artists, and businesses were involved, and monuments became more elaborate and permanent.

Motives were mixed. Alongside remembrance of the dead and prayer for those in uniform, there was, as with the Karbala martyr murals, a concern for recruitment too: memorials could promote ideals of duty and self-sacrifice. On the other hand, and particularly after the war, it was often the Churches that insisted memorials speak of the horror of war, and the need for enduring peace.

The presence of an Established Church perhaps helped the emergence of religious observance in which all could participate, but which retained symbolic power. The central feature of acts of remembrance became two minutes of silence: something in which all could participate with integrity. The distinctive text read at remembrance services is taken from a secular poem. The Cenotaph in London was meant to be a temporary structure, but proved popular, and thus became permanent, partly due to its lack of religious imagery. Religious forms and symbols were broadened and made available to those with widely varying levels of religious commitment. All are united in a need to remember the dead, and to find meaning in loss.

The most striking example of this mingling of Christian imagery with a broadly based need for memorials is the use of the cross in Great War memorials. For Christians the cross symbolizes a particular sacrifice, the death of Christ. In the Great War, however, the meaning of 'great sacrifice' broadened in the minds of many to include the voluntary giving of their lives by soldiers in service of nation. At Christmas 1914 the *Daily Graphic* magazine published a lithograph of James Clark's painting *The Great Sacrifice*, showing a dead soldier's lifeless hand touching the foot of Christ on the cross. The image circulated around the globe, reused in stained glass windows and postcards. The title is deliberately ambiguous. Religious imagery, with its centuries of symbolic weight, overflows into the space left destitute of meaning by war.

By the end of the war, the Imperial War Graves Commission had been set up to formalize memorials to the dead. It commissioned a number of monuments, and one designed by the British architect Reginald Blomfield (1856–1942) emerged as the standard. Known, with the same ambiguity as Clark's lithograph, as 'The Cross of Sacrifice', it became the focal point of British and imperial military cemeteries across the globe (see Figure 2). An austere and classical shape, it marks a break with the romantic Gothic of contemporary church architecture. A bronze sword is superimposed on the stone cross, begging the question 'whose

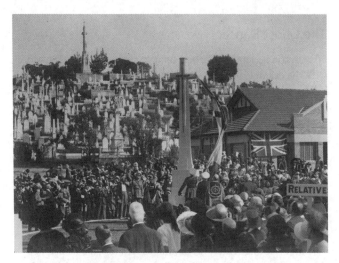

2. Official unveiling of the Cross of Sacrifice at Toowong Cemetery, Brisbane, Australia, on Anzac Day, 1924 by the Governor General, Lord Forster.

sacrifice?' and asking the viewer whether this is a cross adorned with a sword, or a sword supported by a cruciform piece of stone.

Two broad themes emerge as we look at Great War memorials. One is ambiguity. Religious symbols are appropriated and understood in different ways. Religious symbolism of sacrifice and martyrdom can ease sorrows by offering meaning in loss; it can inspire new soldiers to enlist. Related to this ambiguity is the way religious symbolism and war shape one another. Religion provided frames for the remembrance of war. But in this interaction boundaries break down: Otto Dix's *Dresden War Triptych*, for example, uses the form of the triptych which traditionally displays biblical scenes and stands behind the altar in a church. On his triptych Dix captures images of war to prompt memory and reflection in a secular context. As religion engages with war it allows itself to be changed, absorbing new symbols and rituals, its own imagery being appropriated in turn.

The Ghost Dance

We can triangulate the Karbala martyrs and the Cross of Sacrifice with the example of a very different religious movement born out of the heartbreak of war. It is impossible to summarize the story of the Ghost Dance without oversimplifying. Many different cultural forces, emotions, and political factors came together and found expression in it. Its adherents would also have said that something from beyond the visible world was involved. But a central element in the growth of the Ghost Dance was the experience of defeat.

For centuries, the nations of the western part of the American continent had enjoyed freedom to move at will across a vast area of land, never far from a herd of bison offering a ready source of food and clothing. Their way of life was rich in symbolism and ritual, and largely self-contained. In less than a generation in the late 19th century all this came to an end. The land on which the Plains nations had lived, moved, and had their being was settled and fenced. They were confined to reservations too small to support material life, let alone a flourishing culture, the practice of which required space and freedom.

This loss was in essence a military loss. The tribe that displaced them, as tribes had superseded one another across the American continent for thousands of years, was highly mechanized and organized, with an alien way of life. It was a nation of settlers, with a fixed centre, thousands of miles away in Washington DC, its own religion, and manner of life. It was as invincible as it was uncompromising. The people of the plains were outnumbered and outgunned. This was a war with few pitched battles, an early example of the 'asymmetric warfare' that is such a feature of the 21st century. It was an unequal struggle. But it was an armed struggle, still known to history as the Indian Wars. And it was a war in which many once mighty and proud nations went down to defeat.

Among these nations were several related groups inhabiting the Great Basin, the vast and arid territory between the Sierra Nevada and the Rocky Mountains, and known collectively as the Paiute. In the late 1880s, as this defeat was coming to its climax, a Paiute man from Nevada called Wovoka received what he took to be a series of revelations from the spirit world, a divine message of love. In this vision he was given the 'Ghost Dance' as a gift to pass on to his people by means of which they could restore what had been lost. He foresaw that if his people faithfully danced the dance a great flood would sweep away the settlers, the dead would be raised, and the bison would come again.

In his early life Wovoka had worked for a rancher named David Wilson, and had himself been known as Jack Wilson. David Wilson was a Christian and it may be that Wovoka appropriated some aspects of the Christian story and integrated them with his Paiute heritage. The vision he imparted was rich in symbolism. A document known as 'The Messiah Letter', thought to have been dictated by Wovoka, sets out the core of the vision.

> Grandfather says, when your friends die you must not cry. You must not hurt anybody or do harm to anyone. You must not fight...Do not tell the white people about this. Jesus is now upon the earth. He appears like a cloud. The dead are all alive again. I do not know when they will be here...I want everyone to dance every six weeks. Make a feast at the dance and have food that everybody may eat. Then bathe in water. That is all. You will receive good words again from me some time. Do not tell lies.

Wovoka's movement offered a mixture of ethical teaching, hope for a better future, and ritual by means of which the hope was to be realized. The central ritual was the Ghost Dance. It had its roots in an ancient tradition of round dance, the religious aim of which was to secure a safe transition to the next world after death. This ritual had been revived before, as different segments of the indigenous people of what is now the western USA reacted to incursions from the east: the Handsome Lake movement, named after an early 19th-century prophet, looked to the round dance as a part of a rediscovery of traditional values. In Wovoka's movement, however, the Ghost Dance was danced explicitly in the hope that it would lead to the eradication of white dominance of the west.

The Ghost Dance was performed often by hundreds of men and women over several nights, and in many different places as the movement spread from tribe to tribe eastward from Nevada in 1890 (see e.g. Figure 3). It was undoubtedly in part a political movement, a way to bring people together and create the conditions for resistance. But equally undoubted was the spiritual commitment of those involved to something beyond themselves. As the movement gathered pace, participants began to wear decorated 'Ghost Shirts', believing that these shirts would turn away rifle bullets if it came to fighting. In the course of a year, several dozen groups across the Western and Central Plains were drawn into the movement and performed the dance faithfully. The

3. Arapahoes performing the Ghost Dance, 1900, artwork based on photographs by James Mooney.

government in Washington took the view that these gatherings were the prelude to a united armed struggle and assigned over half the territorial army to the area.

At the end of 1890 came the massacre at Wounded Knee Creek, when 350 men, women, and children were killed by a detachment of 500 soldiers in what is generally accepted to have been a catastrophic overreaction to an essentially peaceful gathering. This event marked the end of the Ghost Dance as a mass movement rooted in and expressing a confident religious hope. Native Americans continued to perform the Ghost Dance into the early and mid-20th century, but more and more as a nostalgic curiosity. A 1914 article in the *Nevada State Journal* describes an elderly Wovoka being visited by two equally elderly Paiute chiefs:

> …both show the marks of eighty years and countless ghost dances—the weird ceremony with which the revelations of the Prophet Messiah were celebrated when the excitement was at its height. Both are still the blanket Indians of the plains, and both…travelled the trail…once before—in 1890—coming at that time to secure for their tribes the blessing of the 'Messenger of the Red Men's God' preparatory to the participation of the Cheyenne and Arapahoes in the Indian wars that culminated in the massacre of Wounded Knee…This time the mission…is of a more peaceable nature…they are on their way merely to say a reminiscent 'how' to the Messiah of other days, to talk over with him their memories of the stirring events that his prophecies and his ghost dance caused.

Although written by an outsider, a representative of the victors rather than the defeated, this description does perhaps capture something of the elegiac flavour of the Ghost Dance after Wounded Knee. The Ghost Dance did not die out altogether; indeed in the 1960s some younger Native Americans, feeling that Christianity was too preoccupied with abstractions, sought to revive the Ghost Dance and other traditional forms. But the hope that the Dance would bring restoration of land and freedom, which had energized Wovoka and his disciples, had long since faded. Much religion involves hope embodied in ritual. The ritual can survive after the hope is gone, but not forever.

Meaning and loss

So far we have surveyed three very different situations in which religious resources have been brought to bear on the remembrance of war, and equally have been shaped by it. If, however, the reader has begun to see a clear and regular pattern emerging, then something has gone wrong. For perhaps the one thing that is clear is that the relationship between war and religion is multi-faceted and ambiguous. This may not seem particularly startling; however, if it is true, then it is worth naming. We shall explore different sides of this ambiguity as we go on.

If we confine our gaze to the practice of remembering war, we may see some more specific themes begin to emerge. Many religions are in the business of putting the present moment in the context of eternity. They are thus storehouses of resources for remembering the past and imagining the future. Likewise, religions often deal in that which is hidden beneath and beyond the surface. They are interested not only in phenomena, but in meaning; not only in moments in time, but in the long unfolding story. Religious meanings are of course contestable. Nevertheless, pointing to meaning in events, depicting it, writing, speaking, and singing of it, is a practice in which many religions have grown adept.

These resources of memory and meaning have often been built up over long centuries of performing these tasks. The Ghost Dance, for example, though short-lived as a distinct movement, drew on imagery and ritual thousands of years in the making. And religious resources commonly stem, in different ways, from a commitment to that which is beyond everyday experience. The technical term is 'transcendence'. Reckoning with transcendence over many years gives religions something to offer when the present moment is too large for what it must contain, when the times demand an answer to the question 'why?'

War makes this task of memory and meaning a burning necessity. Those caught up in war have to live in the present moment. Fighting, even simply surviving, demands intense concentration. For those involved, war can be very heavily freighted with experience. Often the experience of war is too large for the short moment in which it is known. Individual soldiers suffering from post-traumatic stress disorder display both a tendency to re-experience the trauma of combat and aberrant memories of events away from the battlefield. The event overflows the space available for memory.

Moreover, war is inherently unpredictable and commonly baffling to the participants. In a historical perspective one may speak of war aims, strategy, victory, and defeat: for the soldier or civilian caught up in it, war is seldom so coherent and purposive. Warfare is often described with some variant of the expression 'long periods of boredom punctuated by moments of sheer terror', but it is not known who coined the phrase. Yet though the events of a war defy attempts to order them into a purposive story, they are of tremendous importance to the people involved. Thus war gives rise both to a deficit of meaning and to an overflow of significance. And what is true for individuals is true for the communities from which they go out to fight.

Little wonder, then, that in the shadow of war, people and societies draw on religious resources. There are proverbially 'no atheists in foxholes' and, again, the originator of this evocative figure of speech is unknown, though it probably dates from the Second World War and from the US armed forces: that many of the perceived insights of war are articulated proverbially perhaps testifies to the universality of the experience. But if it be so that soldiers under fire will often appeal to God for protection, then it is not surprising that when the fighting ceases, many turn to religion to make meaning out of difficult memories.

For some this is a continuation of their existing religious commitment. Others, however, find in religious commitment and practice a new vocabulary for remembering and reflecting. There is ambiguity in this relationship. Religion has sometimes been called upon to celebrate, sometimes to lament war. Religions have placed different values on different wars. This ambiguity is one aspect of a broader ambiguity in the relationship between religion and war, which this book will explore.

One last aspect of this relationship needs to be brought into the foreground at this point: the difference between victory and defeat. The Battle of Karbala has become a powerful religious symbol for followers of Husayn, not followers of Yazid. The Ghost Dance movement came into being in response to a catastrophic loss of power, territory, and life. The Great War, though Britain was nominally among the victors, was a war that left all sides deeply wounded, as was also the case at the end of the Iran–Iraq war, in which the story of Karbala found so many echoes.

Very often the wars which lean most heavily on religious memorialization are wars where the sense of loss predominates. Neither the Napoleonic Wars nor the Second World War gave rise in Britain to the kind of remembrance cult which emerged out of the Great War. Arguably this was because these two wars carried their own meaning which for many was enough. They were, or could be seen as, wars of national survival against an alien power unified under a single fearsome leader bent on invasion, which ended in unequivocal victory. The answer to the question 'why?' on the lips of the bereaved must be easier to frame in such circumstances.

So far we have seen how religion offers to meet the need for meaning in the overwhelming catastrophe of personal and national loss that war brings. We have considered this through looking at religious practices involved in the remembrance of war. In Chapters 2–5 we look at a wider range of situations in which war and religion have shaped one another. We shall see that religions have, at different times and places, motivated and commended war; provided justifications for wars that were fought for other reasons; softened the effects of wars; and offered resources to prevent them. Religions of peace are not always peaceful. Religious wars are not always religious. War can challenge religion, and religion can challenge war.

Chapter 2
Waging holy wars

Warrior gods: warfare and religion in the ancient world

Today we rightly reject the 19th-century notion of religion as progressing toward higher and more rational forms; however, one can discern broad historical changes. Worshipping the God of everything, rather than the god of one's tribe, is more common today than it was 2,000 years ago. By the same token the identification between religion and polity has grown weaker. Two and three thousand years ago the city states and empires that dominated were often those held together by a religious commitment that sanctioned or encouraged warfare.

The tablets known as the *Enuma Elish*, rediscovered in 1849 in the ruins of Nineveh near modern-day Mosul, Iraq, describe the creation of the world as a battle. Tiamat and Apsu are the primal beings. They bring forth the gods. Tiamat repents of giving life to the gods and raises up an army of monsters to fight them. One of them, Marduk, fights Tiamat, and in return is made king of the gods. In the battle between Marduk and Tiamat, in which Marduk is victorious, the world we live in is forged. The tablets on which this epic is written date from the 7th century BCE, but Marduk, and other figures in the myth, appear in the preface to the Code of Hammurabi, a Babylonian law code from the 18th century BCE.

This story was around for a long time. We cannot say for certain how it was understood, nor can we know its impact on the wars fought on and around the Tigris and Euphrates. But it is a worthwhile imaginative effort to enter into the thought world of a religion in which war is a creative act.

This imagery of conflict between different orders of supernatural beings recurs in the Classical Mediterranean world of city states. Here war was a reality of everyday life. Every free man expected to spend part of his life fighting, exposed to the risks of war: death, injury, capture, slavery. Cosmology reflected this experience. Zeus, whom the Romans called Jupiter, obtained his position as mightiest of the gods through battle (see Figure 4). The *Theogony*, by the early Greek poet Hesiod, is a creation myth in which warfare is a constant motif. Classical poets seldom question the morality of violence, but take it to be natural to human existence.

4. Athena battles the giant Alcyoneus in a scene from the *Gigantomachia* (*War of the Giants*). Athena is accompanied by the winged goddess Nike (Victory). Frieze from Great Altar of Zeus in Pergamon (near modern day Bergama, Turkey) now in the Pergamonmuseum, Berlin.

The Greeks did not seek moral example from their gods; they asked for victory. They prepared for battle with religious sacrifices and a search for signs of the gods' favour. Good signs strengthened the will to fight. Part of the spoils of victory was devoted to the gods in their temples.

During the expansion of the Greek states, the oracle at Delphi played a critical role in determining who fought whom, and, by its contribution to morale and unity of purpose, even to who won. The importance of this ritual site grew so great that it became itself the focus of warfare, as different states sought to control it. The integration between the gods and the polity was so thoroughgoing that it scarcely makes sense to distinguish religion from war and say that one motivated the other.

The mingling of state and religion continued with the growth of the Roman Republic and Empire. Ares, a minor god in Greece, became the second god in the Roman pantheon: Mars, the God of War, worshipped by the all-conquering Roman army, and celebrated with his own month, March. Religion protected and validated the army; the army protected and validated religion. The emperors were often generals and often declared to be gods.

As in the European sub-continent, so in the Indian sub-continent, a diverse population divided into numerous communities was shaped by a cosmology in which warfare played a role. India's great epic, the *Mahabharata*, one of the foundational texts of Indian religion, is full of divine heroes and battles. Even the *Bhagavad Gita*, which today is commonly read as a guide to spiritual self-realization, begins with a battle scene, as we shall see in Chapter 4. Although it is hard to make a simple comparison between two such complex thought systems, it is probably fair to say that ethical concerns about war are more prominent in the founding narratives of what we sometimes call 'Hinduism' than in the Greek myths. The martial flavour of the Hindu myths has, however, also sometimes permitted the glorification of war.

In the classical period (300 BCE to 600 CE) warriors and rulers were guided by the *kshatriya-dharma*, the religious ethical code governing the lives of warriors, which justified war and honoured the warrior. The *kshatriya-dharma* embodied a concept of honour, the central pillar of which was that the warrior must fight on and be killed, rather than flee. Warriors were also to fight fairly, and with their equals. A battle well fought could be a form of ritual sacrifice. The victors were sometimes deified. The *kshatriya-dharma* is part of a subtle web of thought about war and peace. In Chapter 4 we will see that it can soften and humanize warfare. But it has also supported the conviction that to lead warriors in battle is a fitting activity for kings. This was particularly so in the late medieval period in India, from the 13th to the 17th centuries, a period when devotion to militant and victorious gods was part of vernacular religion too.

The integration of war and religion was also typical of some ancient civilizations in the Americas. We do not know the detail of their religious lives, but it seems likely that Mayan and Aztec religion was integrated with political life, war and religious practice being deeply intertwined. Some commentators think war was waged for secular reasons such as territorial gain, and its religious character reflected the interpenetration of spiritual forces with every aspect of life. But war often had an annual, ritual quality. Fasting and purification rituals preceded battle; sacrifice of high-ranking prisoners followed victory. In the 16th century, however, these communities were themselves overwhelmed by the more effective military technology of the conquistadors (and perhaps even more by the novel diseases they brought with them to the continent), so that we will never know as much as we would wish about their religion, or their warfare.

Jihad: personal striving or armed struggle?

As we turn now to more modern situations it is worth noting one conceptual distinction when it comes to holy war. Is a particular holy war fought to achieve a religious goal, such as converts or possession of a holy place; or is the war a religious activity in itself? In classical civilizations, as we have seen, it has quite often been the latter. As we move toward the modern world, with its more universal sense of religion, and a less total integration of religion into communal life, the former becomes more of a factor.

Perhaps the most controversial way to raise this question is the case of jihad. If there is one concept in the early 21st century that is the most hotly contested, whose meaning is most open to deeply felt and thoroughly reasoned argument, and to incomprehension and caricature, and on the understanding of which so much hangs, it is jihad. Thus the following condensed treatment must not be read as drawing a conclusion, but as challenging the reader to further exploration.

The Arabic root from which jihad derives is a verb meaning something like 'strive' or 'exert oneself'. As the word developed, it acquired the sense that this striving was against something to which one was opposed.

There are many different objects against which one may strive in jihad, including aspects of one's own character, spiritual powers, the suffering and poverty of others, or a human enemy. Moreover, there are different kinds of striving: one may strive with words against falsehood, or with the will for purity and self-mastery against temptation and weakness: jihad of the tongue; jihad of the heart. The latter is sometimes called the greater jihad, the struggle against the self, the highest expression of the religious life. This inward sense of jihad is widely accepted, and central to the lives of many Muslims. Moreover when directed outward jihad can take many different forms: making donations to charitable causes, helping immigrants, and so on. In recent decades the phrase 'environmental jihad' has gained currency as an expression of the Muslim religious response to climate change.

Jihad spoken of without qualification, however, is classically understood as something like 'warfare with spiritual significance'. Jihad in this sense gets its footing in the Qur'ān at a number of points. Some verses advocate forgiveness of those who oppose the Muslim community; but many unequivocally advocate warfare. 2:191, for example, says 'And slay them wheresoever you come upon them, and expel them whence they expelled you...do not fight with them near the Sacred Mosque until they fight with you there. But if they fight you, then slay them.'

Like any text complex enough to be the cornerstone of a way of life to which billions of people, in diverse ways, are committed, the Qur'ān holds different ideas in tension. There are eirenic verses: 'The servants of the Compassionate are those who walk humbly upon the earth, and when the ignorant address them, say, "Peace"' (25.63) The Qur'ān also places limits on warfare to which we will return in Chapter 4. Verses advocating warfare with the enemies of God are, however, often among those taken to have been revealed later. Qur'ānic interpretation classically uses the principle of abrogation: if two verses appear to conflict, that which was revealed later is given priority. There is also a large body of hadith (sayings and acts of the Prophet) that encourage war in support of Islam.

There is, then, a solid basis for what one might call 'holy war' in the texts of Islam: the Qur'ān places limits on war, but within those limits war is sanctioned or enjoined. Islam is highly diverse, however, and within that diversity, different communities at different times have lived this out in very different ways. It is not helpful to speak in terms of 'evolution' here, either, as though there were an ideal of jihad toward which all must progress. Ideas change, and change back. New understandings emerge, old understandings lie dormant and resurface. To give a very brief mountain-top review of this complex history it will be helpful, however, to think in terms of three periods: the early centuries of expansion and conquest; a longer middle period when there was a political reality to the worldwide Muslim community; and the modern period, beginning with the break-up of the Ottoman Empire.

Beginnings and conquest

In returning to the origins of jihad it is important to note that warfare had a central role in the early development of Islam. Islam begins with the initial revelation to the Prophet Muhammad in 610. The first thirteen years are characterized by oppression and migrations. But 623 saw the beginning of military action by the new Muslim community. Victory in the Battle of Badr, which sura 3 of the Qur'ān describes as a gift of God, and the victories which followed, formed the early Muslim identity. These early battles were the start of a military and religious expansion that unfolded rapidly in Islam's first two centuries.

The period from 634 to 742 is often called the Islamic Age of Conquest. The Prophet had died in 632. His successors pursued an energetic campaign from their heartlands around Mecca and Medina. This brought them into conflict with the Christian Byzantine Empire in the West, centred on Constantinople, and the Sasanian Empire, predominantly Zoroastrian, its heartlands to the east in Persia. The Sasanian Empire was completely wiped out, and the Byzantines lost all their African territories and all but the western end of what is now Turkey. As the Umma, the worldwide political and religious community of Muslims, expanded, conquered peoples converted and assimilated, and became themselves frontline shock troops. By the mid-8th century a crescent from the Pyrenees through North Africa, the Middle East, and Arabia to the Hindu Kush was under Muslim rule. Under this rule, it is important to note, other religions, particularly Christianity, continued to flourish.

The case can certainly be made that this expansion was a holy war. It is historically continuous with the beginning of Islam. There were not yet clearly established distinct dynasties, nations, and empires all professing Islam. The schism between Shi'a and Sunni Islam was only taking shape. In the period of conquest one can conceive of the whole Muslim world as a single Umma defined by, and making common cause around, religious ideals of which warfare is at least an important part. *Kitab al-Jihad*, by Abdallah b. Al-Mubarak (d. 797), is a good example. An important early articulation of the concept of jihad, it records sayings of the Prophet inviting the reader to take on himself the mantle of a defender of Islam. It articulates the idea of the sinning but repentant believer for whom skilful fighting with pure motives washes away sin. Whatever other motives may also have been in play, many of the people of the time took themselves to be fighting a holy war.

Caliphate and consolidation

By the 9th century the pace of expansion had slowed. Islam continued to spread eastward, but more gradually, driven by trade and missionary activity. The western and northern borders of Islam now marched with the boundaries of a newly energized Christendom. For the first time Muslims had to recognize that the era of total conversion to, or domination by, Islam was not coming in this lifetime. The apocalyptic strain in Islam became muted. The world was no longer divided into *dar al-Islam* (abode of Islam/peace/monotheism) and *dar al-harb* (abode of war).

As the conquest lost momentum, enthusiasm for the practice of the classical jihad of the sword declined. In its place arose a keener interest in the theory of jihad as a peaceful religious practice. By the 12th century many theologians distinguished a 'greater' and a 'lesser' jihad. This has its roots in the hadith, though some of the key texts are disputed. The lesser jihad is the necessary evil of warfare. The greater jihad is the multi-faceted spiritual struggle toward personal purity, submission to God, service to the community, and defence of the faith by preaching, writing, and example. In time this newer sense of jihad came to have far the greater impact on the lives of practitioners.

The literature of the lesser jihad also broadened and deepened, giving more detail to the principles that govern and limit warfare. Some came to see conquest as less legitimate than defence, and many of the wars fought by Muslim powers in that period were indeed defensive. Warfare did not cease to be part of the understanding of jihad. But the jihad of the sword became a task for the state, for rulers, and for the military class.

Modernity: fragmentation and reassessment

The last few centuries, however, have seen a steep decline in Muslim political power. It is much easier now than 500 years ago to see Islam as embattled and threatened. Until the dissolution of the Ottoman Empire in the aftermath of the Great War, a Muslim could think of the lesser jihad as a matter for the military authorities of the Umma. Since then, Muslims have faced the theoretical challenge of personal responsibility for the jihad of the sword. Moreover, the rise of secular materialism can act as a reminder of the situation of the earliest Muslim community, a lone voice proclaiming monotheism in a world of idol worshippers.

All this prompted a rethinking of jihad. Many took the view that fighting was no longer required, if it ever had been. The focus was now solely on the greater jihad of personal purity. Through the 20th and 21st centuries the concept continued to expand to include a notion of civic jihad. For others, however, the two centuries leading up to 1920 brought the jihad of the sword back into focus. Since the late 18th century, revivalist movements had started to respond to erosion of Muslim power by calling for a return to the ancient faith. This often meant the establishment of Muslim territory by means of warfare.

The most geopolitically significant jihad of the long 19th century was the Wahhabist movement in the Arabian peninsula. Begun by the jurist and theologian Muhammad ibn Abd al-Wahhab (1703–91) as a campaign against idolatry and Sufism, it led to the establishment of Saudi Arabia. The constitution of Saudi Arabia today affirms that 'Government in Saudi Arabia derives power from the Holy Quran and the Prophet's tradition.' The flag displays the words 'there is but one God and Muhammad is His Prophet' over an image of a sword.

Wahhabism has been firmly on the world's agenda since 9 September 2001. Fifteen of the nineteen men who hijacked and crashed four aeroplanes in the USA on that day were subjects of the Saudi Kingdom, as was the instigator of the attack, Osama bin Laden. It should go without saying that their actions are at odds with the attitudes of a huge majority of Muslims. Nevertheless, it is hard to deny that considerations of ultimate values were part of what drove them. It will be helpful to delve a little into the specific detail of these concerns as they came together in the 20th century. This period saw the growth of groups that set themselves against secular modernity, foremost among them the Muslim Brotherhood in Egypt and the Jamaat-al-Islami in India.

A good starting point for understanding these developments is the thought of Sayyid Qutb, a leading member of the Muslim Brotherhood. His key book is *Milestones*, published in 1964, which he wrote whilst in prison for political conspiracy; he was later re-arrested and executed in 1966. Qutb discusses jihad in the context of the foundational period of Islam, the thirteen years when Muhammad 'called people to God through preaching, without fighting…' After this time followed migration, and divine permission to fight. Qutb affirms Sura 2.256 'There is no coercion in religion.' But this does not entail dispensing with force, for one has to understand the use of force in a non-modernist way:

> Jihad has no relationship to modern warfare, either in its causes or
> in the way in which it is conducted. The causes of Islamic Jihad
> should be sought in the very nature of Islam and its role in
> the world.

For Qutb, Islam is a proclamation of the kingship of God, and
thus a declaration of freedom from human kingship. This calls for
a twofold approach: preaching to help human beings acknowledge
freely the authority of God; 'the movement' to attack the human,
political obstacles to living freely under God.

> It is not the intention of Islam to force its beliefs on people, but
> Islam is not merely 'belief'...[it is]...a declaration of the freedom
> of man from servitude to other men. Thus it strives from the
> beginning to abolish all those systems and governments which are
> based on the rule of man over men.

Conversion comes through persuasion, reason, and example, all
aspects of the greater jihad. But force is vital nevertheless. Because
all people, Muslim or non-Muslim, who live under human rule are
not free. There is a religious imperative to liberate them into the
one state for which humankind is fitted: the rule of God.

This is what Muslim warriors have always fought for in Qutb's
view. He tells the story of three Muslim warriors from the age of
conquest who are asked by a Persian general why they were
fighting. They answer, Qutb says, 'God has sent us to bring anyone
who wishes from servitude to men into the service of God alone.'
The lesser jihad is indeed about warfare, and this war is a religious
duty. But it is not a war to force adherence to Islam. It is thus a
holy war, but not in the way the secular world understands. The
whole concept is hard to grasp without entering into the religious
outlook in which it was forged.

Qutb's thought has been very influential since his death. And he is
one of a number of thinkers advocating return to the original

sources of faith. A key impact has been to give modern currency to the jihad of the sword. The Afghan war of resistance against the Soviet Union was fought by groups mostly describing themselves as *Mujahideen*—cognate with jihad. These implacable fighters who brought the Red Army to its knees certainly took jihad to be more than inner striving for personal purity. As the Berlin Wall fell in the same year the Red Army retreated across the Oxus, this jihad arguably had a larger geopolitical impact than any since the Middle Ages.

Crusades and wars of religion

Ironically the subtle classical understanding of the jihad of the sword, which moderates war as well as motivating it, was given a sharp focus by a collision with another form of religious war. Ali ibn Tahir al-Sulami, a Muslim scholar who lived through the First Crusade, wrote of this catastrophic event as a Christian jihad.

The crusades is the name given to the series of campaigns launched by Western European powers between the late 11th and the early 16th century to contest control of the Holy Land, and to suppress threats to Western Christianity on the continent of Europe. Like any major historical movement, the crusades are easier to classify and define in hindsight than they probably were at the time. They began with a clear focus on Jerusalem, a holy place for Jews, Christians, and Muslims, then part of the empire of the Seljuqs, a Turkic people practising Sunni Islam, whose territory stretched from the Caucasus to the Bosporus. A commonly referenced starting point is the Council of Clermont in 1095. Pope Urban II declared that anyone who fought to bring Jerusalem under Christian control would be obeying the command of Jesus Christ (Mark 8: 34 and parallels) to 'deny himself, and take up his cross, and follow me'. Several tens of thousands of people responded. Their symbol was the cross. The Latin for cross being *crux*, the movement came to be known as the crusade.

This was not a war fought by an organized state. Rather, bands and small armies of different sizes came together for a common purpose in response to a call by religious leaders. Some were disciplined units under the command of a feudal lord. Some were rabbles of individuals with little or no military experience. Many died on the way to the Holy Land. But in 1099 they captured Jerusalem with great violence, and the city remained in the hands of Christian rulers, not always at peace with one another, until 1187.

Pope Eugenius III launched a second crusade in 1147, calling not only for attacks on parts of the Holy Land still under Muslim rule, but also for an intensification of the push to conquer, or reconquer, the Muslim regions of what is now Spain. This Second Crusade ended with inconclusive defeat in the Holy Land, whilst giving impetus to the ultimate Christian victory in the Iberian peninsula (Figure 5).

The Third Crusade was a response to the recapture of Jerusalem by Muslim forces under Saladin, in 1187. This crusade was better organized, led by the Holy Roman Emperor and the King of England. But it did not succeed in taking Jerusalem. The Fourth Crusade, begun in 1202, became a conflict among Christians, as the Western, Catholic crusaders sacked the Eastern, Orthodox capital of Byzantium (now Istanbul) in 1204 en route to the Holy Land. Jerusalem remained in the hands of Muslim powers, apart from a short negotiated period of Christian occupation in the 13th century, until towards the end of the First World War.

Popes continued to call for crusades, but from the mid-13th century these were no longer aimed at displacing Muslim forces from Jerusalem. Instead the target was minority Christian and other religious groups within Western and Central Europe who were perceived as threats to the integrity of the Catholic Church. Jewish communities were often the victims. The crusading period

5. One of many medieval maps of Jerusalem (*c.*1170, when the city was under crusader control) illustrating the significance of the Holy City. The crusader, holding a shield emblazoned with a red cross, drives his opponents off the field, away from the city gates and the sacred spaces of Jerusalem.

petered out in the 16th century, as religious and military energy was absorbed by the Reformations and the internal European wars that followed.

What was it that drove generation after generation of crusaders to endure danger and to fight for many years, often with terrible violence? Perhaps one of the strongest motives was remission of sins. The century or two prior to the crusades had seen the development of the *Pax Dei* ('peace of God')—a movement of the Church progressively limiting scope for violence. A network of proclamations and decrees prescribed what could be done to non-combatants in war. Feudal landowners were encouraged to swear oaths forsaking violence. All this was in the context of religious teaching often drawing on the example of non-violent self-sacrifice offered by Christ. The impact on the knights, who constituted what we would now call a class of professional soldiers, was profound. In this age of deeply felt piety, those whose calling and skill was to bear arms laboured under a heavy burden of guilt. Pope Urban's promise at the Council of Clermont that all who died on the crusade would receive 'complete remission of their sins' offered a way out.

There is good evidence for the states of mind (perhaps 'soul' would be better) of some of these warriors as they set out. Before leaving their lands, many drew up charters to dispose of their property in their absence. The charters usually begin with a preamble in which they say why they are going on the crusade. Often what drives them is the hope of forgiveness of sins, for themselves and their ancestors, or to revenge an insult to God. One French nobleman settling his affairs before leaving on the Second Crusade writes thus:

> I, Arnold Seschaves, being solicitous for the salvation of the souls of myself and my parents and mindful that on the Last Day, when at the advent of our Lord Jesus Christ all men must rise again with their bodies and be ready to account for their deeds, those who did

good deeds will go to eternal life but those who did evil deeds to eternal fire, in order that my Lord the Blessed Peter, to whom God gave the power of binding and loosing and the keys to the celestial kingdom, may deign to open the doors of the celestial kingdom to myself and my father and my mother and other ancestors of my family, gave him my land at La Groux...

This was a time in which the younger sons of landowning families were going into monasteries. Their brothers who remained on the land as feudal chieftains shared their piety. They certainly took on the guilt which that piety brought with it for a soldier. Some even explicitly combined piety with warrior virtue, founding the order of Poor Fellow-Soldiers of Christ and of the Temple of Solomon, recognized by the Pope in 1139 and popularly known as the Knights Templar. Its fighting members were some of the most skilful soldiers of the crusades, who wore a distinctive white habit reminiscent of those worn by monks. One could go so far as to describe the crusades as being, for some, an armed pilgrimage.

This view, that the crusades were very much a holy war, motivated by deep religious commitment, is not the only one. There is an argument that the crusades were rooted in economics and realpolitik. In this perspective, from the 8th to the 15th century two geopolitical powers, the Catholic Christians of Western Europe and the Muslims of Arabia and West-Central Asia, vied for territorial dominance. As part of this struggle, successive popes hired mercenaries with promises of new lands if they could conquer them, and sent them to take the fight to the enemy, just as Muslim armies had acquired territory in the Iberian Peninsula.

Against this argument it is worth noting that the crusades were, in the final balance, financial loss-makers. Indeed, the same charters in which the crusaders express their piety also speak of worries about how they are going to pay for the enterprise. Moreover, if the crusades were a global political clash between rival power blocs, then the focus on sites of religious, rather than strategic, significance needs explanation. Perhaps the popes knew they could get religiously minded laymen to fight for Jerusalem but not for Ancyra (modern-day Ankara). But then the least one can say is that a deeply felt piety was centrally involved.

The crusades cast a long shadow. After the 9/11 attacks, President George W. Bush spoke of a 'crusade' against terrorism. The use of the term passed largely without notice in the United States, but in Europe and the Middle East, where the history of the crusades is written in the physical geography, it caused alarm. Chris Kyle, a US special forces soldier who served several tours in Iraq, and whose story was told in the film *American Sniper* (2014, directed by Clint Eastwood), recalled in his autobiography of the same name, 'On the front of my arm, I had a Crusader cross inked in. I wanted everyone to know I was a Christian.'

Other holy wars

As we shall see in Chapter 3, sometimes economic, personal, geopolitical factors do indeed dominate wars with religious features. And even in the two examples we have looked at here, other forces than religion were at work. Nevertheless, these wars took their shape and driving force from the religions professed by those who fought them. And the aims with which they were fought were explicitly religious aims. Thus, in the terms we have been using, it would be fair to call them 'holy wars'.

History offers many other examples. Jewish resistance to imperialism in the Classical period, first against the Seleucid Empire that succeeded Alexander the Great's conquests, and then to the Romans, had a strong religious motivation which gave it a persistence which most other subject peoples did not maintain. The English Civil War, and the smaller conflicts surrounding it, were rooted in deeply committed disagreements over religion. Sikhism, though originating in an eirenic universalism, was forced by its geographical location at the margin between the Hindu and

Muslim worlds to develop a strong martial tradition. The same factors have also often made the Sikh community the object of violence itself.

A case can even be made that the First World War, rather than being the first unequivocally modern war, was rather the last of Europe's religious wars. We have seen how religion was a source of solace to the bereaved (Chapter 1). Religion was also central to the rhetoric motivating both sides. Patriotism and spiritual commitment overlapped in the hearts and minds of those who fought. English bishops wrote of the Allies as 'predestined instruments to save the Christian civilisation of Europe' and declared the Church's duty to 'mobilize the nation for holy war'. German Lutheran pastors and professors hymned the world war that would 'transfigure our nature, like the Word and the Spirit', or prayed, 'Bless this war, if it brings to our people the religious uplifting which makes us unconquerable.'

Holy wars: holy and unholy

The question whether any given war was a holy war, or a secular war that exploited religion as rallying cry, will always be a contested one. But before we reflect upon it, there is one other issue to consider, for many the most important question one can ask about war and religion. It is the question whether a war is not merely motivated and energized by a religion, but also a fitting expression of that religion. Is it consistent with the principles of the religion, or merely a deeply felt but wrong use of those principles? Is it, as well as being a holy war, also in religious terms holy?

To take one example of pressing contemporary relevance: very many Muslims would make the case that whilst Daesh (ISIS) and Al-Qaeda may have a deeply felt religious motivation, their warfare is not a correct expression of Islam. Faith may well be at work, particularly in the case of the 9/11 attackers: warfare from which there is no victorious homecoming is more likely to be fought by soldiers for whom death is not conclusive. At the same time, most Muslim scholars argue this is not jihad in the full sense, of war within judicious and humane limits. The commitment and courage of jihad is present: but the destruction of the World Trade Center violates limits which jihad places on war, to which we return in Chapter 4. Likewise the fighters of Daesh in Northern Iraq, though surely motivated by faith, failed the test of jihad, even as articulated by Qutb, by forcing the conversion of Christian communities. Indeed many jurists argue that the wars of Daesh were not authorized by the pronouncement of a legitimate imam, so that they were not jihad but rebellion or disorder.

Drawing a distinction between holy wars that really are holy in the terms of the religion in the name of which they are fought, and holy wars that grow out of a distortion of religion, is always going to be controversial. In many cases it will be a matter on which there will perhaps never be a consensus. This is in part because it is a matter on which it is hard for a purely academic opinion to get a footing: a view on whether an action is truly 'holy' will almost inevitably rest on a level of religious commitment. Thus it is a question that takes us beyond the scope of this book. But it is a key aspect of the debate, of which we must at least be aware. It is a question that resurfaces again and again, and those interested in religion and war in anything other than an entirely abstract and academic sense must face it, one way or another.

Chapter 3
Sanctifying secular wars

In Chapter 2 we examined some wars that could be described as fundamentally religious in character: not only are the fighters motivated by religious commitment, but the purposes and conduct of the war are religious. We distinguished between wars that are forms of religious expression in themselves, and those fought to make converts, capture holy places, or achieve other religious aims. And we noted the possibility that a genuinely religious war could yet be challenged by the religion that gave it birth: that it could be a holy war but not holy.

Many wars in which religion is involved are, however, not holy wars in any of these senses. In this chapter we look at another category of religious war: wars in which religious commitment is used to pursue aims largely unrelated to religion.

The dividing line between the wars we consider in this chapter and the religious wars of Chapter 2 is highly contested and moves back and forth as historiographical fashions change. Religious explanations of the crusades were popular in the 19th century. With the strengthening of Marxism and economics as the interpretative frame for history, power and money became the driving forces. The pendulum has swung the other way again since 1989. Nevertheless, reading history from the vantage point of a relatively secular world can colour our perceptions. We need an imaginative effort to enter into the heart and mind of Henry V, who heard Mass three times in succession before Agincourt. The world in which we live predisposes us to underestimate the religious content of war in the past. If in doubt, then, it probably *was* a holy war.

There have also, though, been many religious wars that did not fit this pattern. We can argue about precisely *where* to draw the line, but a distinction can helpfully be made between wars fought for religious purposes and wars whose objectives and motives are not religious even if the slogans and passions are. This chapter describes situations where religion has been the flag of convenience, the fig leaf, or even the fuel, for wars fought for essentially secular reasons.

Japan, Shinto, and Buddhism in the Second World War

Many commentators have drawn parallels between the 9/11 atrocities and the Japanese attack on Pearl Harbor in 1941, which signalled Japanese and American entry into the Second World War. Both were surprise attacks that shocked and galvanized America. And there is another powerful image that resonates in both scenes: the plane crash as weapon of war. Although it was not until later in the Second World War that formal kamikaze units were formed of pilots committed to crashing their planes into enemy ships, even at Pearl Harbor at least some pilots of damaged planes, rather than bail out, intentionally aimed their planes at strategic targets.

As with the pilots and suicide bombers of Al-Qaeda, the motives of the kamikaze pilots must remain to a degree inscrutable, for if they succeed it is then much harder to find evidence of their motivations: but some motivation that goes well beyond narrow self-interest must be at work, and this may well have a religious character. More broadly, Japanese soldiers betrayed an almost unimaginable determination not to surrender. In the battle for Iwo Jima, for example, scarcely more than 200 of the 20,000 soldiers in the Japanese garrison were taken prisoner, and most of these were captured whilst unconscious. A pragmatic fear of the consequences of surrender is unlikely to explain this fully.

Kamikaze is a word associated with Shinto, a religion with a deep history in Japan which acquired in the mid-20th century the reputation of being a religion of war. It is easy on a superficial reading of this history to think of Japanese military aggression in that period as a form of holy war. But a more balanced view requires context. Shinto is not a religion that emphasizes a unified, written philosophy, or complex technical theology, or formal hierarchical structures. Scriptures are relatively unimportant. Rather, Shinto is rich in ritual, in shrines, and in deities. The latter are known as *kami*. *Kami* may be powerful ancestral forces, they may be the spirits of mighty storms and other natural forces, or they may be the spirits of everyday objects particular to a village or a hillside: streams, boulders, and trees. There is then nothing fundamental in Shinto to make its adherents particularly warlike. Shinto has a local, pastoral flavour, celebrating the particular, rooted in nature and community.

Shinto offers relatively little in the way of formal ethical teaching: thus, though there is no pacifist ethic, neither is there any general commandment to war or conquest. Hachiman, a popular deity, appeared to early outside observers to be a Shinto 'god of war'. In reality he is better described as a god of warriors. The most celebrated Shinto military success was a defensive deliverance from invasion. On two occasions in the 13th century, Mongol invasion fleets from mainland Asia were destroyed by typhoons, and these winds (*kaze*) came to be worshipped as of divine origin—the *Kamikaze*.

It was after the Meiji Restoration, the political upheavals that followed the sudden opening of Japan to Western trade in the

1860s, that a series of political decisions helped to codify and reify Shinto as a discrete 'religion' distinct from Buddhism, and then to posit shrine rites as separate from religion and part of the official, secular, rituals of the state. Part of the strategy of the Meiji regime was to define what counted as religion and what did not, in a way that supported its state aims. Shrines were initially treated as discrete religious institutions, then as non-religious institutions with state funding; funding was then withdrawn, and in 1900 jurisdiction over shrines and 'religions' was taken over by the government.

After the 1904–5 war in which Japan inflicted a humiliating defeat on Russia, the Japanese war dead were themselves enshrined, as the dead of earlier wars had been. The government further sought to make shrines orderly, reducing the number to one per village, to fit them within a national structure. Imperial servants were sent to the nation's shrines in 1914 to announce the entry of Japan into the First World War. From the 1890s onward Japan progressively invaded parts of the East Asian continent, beginning with Taiwan and continuing with Korea and then, from the 1930s, Manchuria. As this expansion continued further shrines were established at which the conquered were obliged to worship. This attempt to mobilize the deeply felt emotional power of Shinto, rooted in the soil of the Japanese islands, to focus an aggressive and expansionist patriotism, reached its zenith in the Second World War (Figure 6).

This was, though, no holy war. In the first place, it was certainly not the outworking of Shinto itself. Shinto historically has never been a religion which demands to be expressed in warfare. Neither, though, was this a war for religious objectives. The making of converts was not an end in itself, and indeed the concept of conversion to a universally valid faith scarcely translates from Western monotheism into Shinto, which is so thoroughly a religion of the particular. And by the same token there is no one holy place for which the armies in a holy war can

6. Men in Japanese Imperial uniform at the Yasukuni Shrine in Tokyo, Japan, 15 August 2019, the 74th anniversary of Japan's surrender in the Second World War. Founded by the Japanese Emperor in 1869, it commemorates those killed in Japanese service from the 19th century up to the First Indochina War of 1946–54. Since the end of the Second World War it has frequently been a site of controversy.

contend. Shinto shrines abound in the infinite variety of nature and village life.

Moreover it is important to note that not only Shinto, but Buddhism and indeed Christianity, cooperated with the Japanese state to foster unity of national purpose and sustain a martial spirit. Indeed, if there was a thread in Japan's religious cloth that had over centuries leant itself to militarism it was—and this is a very good example of the protean nature of religion—Buddhism.

Buddhism originated against the background of early Hinduism, in the life and teaching of Siddhartha Gautama, a nobleman who renounced his status to become a spiritual guide in the north-east of what we now know as India, some time around the 5th century BCE. Central to his teaching was the practice of detachment: not that the daily concerns of human life, from politics to pain, were malign or worthy of contempt, but that they were not ultimate realities, and need not be permitted to have mastery. Instead, he commended as our ultimate aspiration *nirvana*, a Sanskrit word meaning literally 'blowing out'—the extinguishing of attachment, giving rise to a blissful calm impervious to any earthly event. As Buddhist practice spread it acquired distinctive characteristics in the different places it took root. So for example Theravada Buddhism flourishes in Sri Lanka, Myanmar, and Thailand. Further east, under the broad heading of Mahayana Buddhism, several schools proliferate. The Buddhist tradition in China, Japan, and Korea is sometimes distinguished as *Chan*, *Zen*, and *Son*—a common root meaning something like 'meditation'.

This outlook can indeed provide resources for pacifism. If territory, prosperity, national pride, and life itself are only illusions, then to inflict pain and suffering to preserve them is unnecessary. But as we shall see, Buddhists have fought their fair share of wars, and the concepts and practices of Buddhism can also resource the warrior in powerful ways.

In Japan Zen was early adopted by the Samurai, the warrior caste that frequently dominated Japanese politics in the second millennium. They particularly valued the self-discipline and techniques of detachment taught by Buddhism. As early as the 13th century the Japanese Regent Hojo Tokimune undertook training in Zen as preparation for resisting an anticipated Mongol invasion—the same invasion that was then driven back by the *Kamikaze* typhoons. He, and the warriors who came after him, found in Zen a detachment that made them fearless of death in battle, the power of concentrating and remaining calm under stress, the cultivation of swift intuitive action, and an ethic of simple living that contributed to the distinctive Samurai *esprit de corps*.

The apogee of this use of religion for warlike purposes might be the intriguing figure of Lt Col. Sugimoto Goro (1900–37) who died in battle in China. He was the author of *Taigi* ('Great Duty'), a book on military duty and Zen that was widely published after his death. Sugimoto's statement of his Zen commitment is a striking illustration of the warlike potential in Buddhist thought and practice:

> Through my practice of Zen I am able to get rid of my ego. In facilitating the accomplishment of this, Zen becomes, as it is, the true spirit of the imperial military.

This warrior ethic, with its roots in the Buddhism imported into Japan from northern India, played a larger part in shaping the Japanese military into a dedicated and implacable fighting force in the first half of the 20th century than did the Shinto of the Japanese countryside. A policy statement by the occupying armies after the Second World War asserted that 'the Shinto faith properly directed need not be dangerous'. This statement probably reflects a desire to reframe Shinto for political reasons, much as the Meiji had sought to do. But there may also be a kernel of truth here. Perhaps the key word is 'directed'. Without a formal hierarchy or an articulated creed, Shinto may have been particularly vulnerable to co-option.

The sudden opening up of Japan in the 1860s posed huge challenges and offered considerable opportunities to Japan's rulers. Distinguishing between religious and secular motives is difficult and controversial, but it is a job that needs to be attempted. And it does seem at least arguable that the motives for building up the Japanese state and its economy from a feudal level to the point where Japan could dominate a global hemisphere, were not religious motives: at least not to the same degree as the crusades and the early Islamic wars of conquest were religiously motivated. Nevertheless, to achieve such a position of dominance in less than a century Japan's rulers had to call in aid whatever natural, economic, or cultural resources were to hand. This included making the most of the imagery, practices, and pre-existing commitment of Buddhism and Shinto, both suitably brought under state control.

Intercommunal warfare

In the case of early 20th-century Japan, to simplify a very complex story, religion, skilfully manipulated by those in power, was a useful element in a broad ideological effort to focus the energies of a nation for war. The Japanese example, however, is in some ways an outlier. Shinto and Buddhism helped strengthen the Japanese war effort. But Japan fought a war of outward conquest. More often, when religion supports rather than motivates war, this is in situations where two religions, each related to a community more or less defined in other ways, collide.

This dynamic has been present in many terrible wars of the last few centuries. It can arguably be seen at work in Ireland (particularly Northern Ireland), in Greece, in the lands through which the Tigris and the Euphrates run, and in the Balkans, Kashmir, and Sri Lanka. A similar pattern is often repeated: communal identities, perhaps involving shared language or history, but often without established institutions; religions replete with powerful shared symbolism; skilful leaders who use the religious commitment to bolster a sense of unity and belligerence against the other.

The Kosovo myth

Particularly illustrative is the case of Serbia. For many centuries the Balkans have been inhabited in part by people speaking variants of a common language, Serbian, and often adhering to the Serbian Orthodox Church. There was a sense of common identity but no history of self-government: rule emanated from beyond, from the Ottoman or Habsburg empires. The 19th century was a time of growing interest in nationalism, in customs and history linked to people and places. This was a matter sometimes of rediscovery, sometimes of invention, in practice usually both. A key trope in the formation of Serbian identity was the Battle of Kosovo Polje (1389). At Kosovo Polje the Ottoman Empire inflicted a defeat on a Serbian army; in the centuries that followed Kosovo became a predominantly Muslim province.

In the 19th century, an essentially mythical set of meanings was attached to this historical battle. The symbolism of heroic defeat in defence of Christendom was strengthened by the drawing of parallels with the Crucifixion. Serb nationalists speaking of the rebirth of 'Greater Serbia' consciously echoed the Resurrection. Thus the most compelling symbols of a deeply felt faith came to be associated with a nationalist project. The horror of the Crucifixion and the reality of the Resurrection can be deeply felt realities for the Christian; co-opting these commitments for political ends is thus a strong move. Several dramatic depictions of the Battle of Kosovo Polje date from this period (see e.g. Figure 7).

In a speech to mark the 600th anniversary of the battle, Slobodan Milošević said,

> The Kosovo heroism has been inspiring our creativity for 6 centuries, and has been feeding our pride and does not allow us to forget that at one time we were an army great, brave, and proud, one of the few that remained undefeated when losing.

This was explicitly to recall the role—perhaps a mythical role—of Serbs as the 'front line' of Christendom against Muslim expansion westward after the crusades. The following decade saw increasing military violence (in which few parties were blameless) culminating in a war over Kosovo between NATO and the former Yugoslavia, now in essence 'Greater Serbia'.

7. **Painting of the Battle of Kosovo Polje, 15 June 1389: Prince Lazar, leader of the Serbian army, is pictured dying with his horse. This image was painted in 1870, by Adam Stefanović, at a time of rekindled interest in Serbian nationalism—the painting is thus as much an appropriation of the battle for contemporary purposes, as a representation of a historic event.**

The rhetorical use of the Battle of Kosovo Polje, and its blending with the Christian narrative, is a particularly clear example of the co-option of deeply felt religion to promote a war that is not in itself primarily religious. But in different ways across time and space the pattern repeats itself frequently.

Northern Ireland: colonial or sectarian?

It is true that the tension between Protestant and Catholic had been embedded in Irish politics at least since the mid-17th century, if not from the Reformation (Figure 8). On the other hand the tension between native and incomer goes back at least to the 11th century and the arrival of the Normans, who, though ultimately descended from Viking invaders of northern France, were by then co-religionists with the Irish. Colonization of Ireland from England goes back several centuries before the distinction between Protestant and Catholic was ever thought of.

8. Mural in Shankill Parade, West Belfast, depicting Oliver Cromwell (1599–1658), Lord Protector of England, after his victory in the Civil War, whose campaigns in Ireland have been celebrated by Protestants as an assertion of their rights against the Catholic majority. There is no evidence that the words attributed to Cromwell on this mural were said or written by him, and his actual pronouncements were not religiously extremely sectarian: he was probably more anti-clerical than anti-Catholic.

Likewise, the struggle for Irish independence from Britain was in the 18th century a thoroughly ecumenical affair. The Society of United Irishmen was central to the Irish rebellion of 1798 in which the cause of Irish independence was backed by secular revolutionary France. The founder of the United Irishmen was Theobald Wolfe Tone (1763–98), a descendant of Protestant Huguenot refugees, and brought up in the (Protestant) Church of Ireland.

Yet in the 20th century a very clear identification between Protestantism and Union with Britain, on one hand, and Catholicism and the aspiration of a united and independent Ireland, was well established. The paramilitary organizations that fought for and against Northern Ireland remaining part of the UK had a clear religious dividing line between them. The Ulster

Defence Association (UDA) was Protestant, whilst the Irish Republican Army (IRA) was Catholic. Both had secular members, aims, and methods; their identities, however, were often articulated in religious terms. Until a few decades ago it was not uncommon to hear supporters of football teams associated with Protestantism chanting 'UDA, on our way, fuck the Pope and the IRA.'

Sudan

We have already seen (Chapter 2) how movements of Islamic renewal, with a drive toward the purity of the ancient faith, took hold in many parts of the Muslim world in the 18th and 19th centuries, as the power and coherence of the worldwide Muslim community declined. That which has had the most widely felt impact was Wahhabist revival in the Arabian peninsula. Two others that have continued to echo down the decades were the evanescent Mahdist state in late 19th-century Sudan, and the more long-lived Sokoto caliphate in northern Nigeria. Both were, to begin with, the expression of deeply held and militantly expressed religious faith. By the 20th century, however, they had become enmeshed in the ethnic and economic web of politics in their respective parts of Africa.

At independence Sudan had no natural borders or established common values. It had been a subsidiary imperial possession under Egypt, which had been part of the Ottoman Empire and then dominated by Britain. Moreover the divide between north and south had been deepened by British imperial policies. An educated Arabic-speaking elite in the north stepped into administrative positions, whereas in the south the social infrastructure was not actively developed: education and other services were confided to the care of Christian missionaries.

In the 1950s southerners wished to delay independence so that the south could become viable as an independent nation, but decolonization went ahead on schedule. Ruled from Khartoum by a Muslim, Arabic-speaking governing class closer to neighbours across the Red Sea than to the sub-Saharan hinterland, Sudan became increasingly divided. The missionary schools in the south were taken over by the government and the official day of rest changed from Sunday to Friday, as Khartoum endeavoured to forge a national unity based on Arabization and Islamization. This contributed to a state of chronic civil war in Sudan which has unfolded in several different phases, whose boundaries in time and space are conflicted.

In 1973 a new constitution enshrined the place of Christianity and tribal religions in the nation's life, but was more honoured in the breach than in the observance. In the same decade tensions were intensified by two important liquids. The government proposed a canal to divert water from the southern wetlands to the Nile near Khartoum; and oil was found under the northern part of south Sudan. By the 1980s north and south (the latter itself ununited) were at war.

In 1989 a coup brought General Omar Bashir to power, who pursued a radical Islamist agenda and gave support to Osama bin Laden and other militants. Several million Sudanese, mostly southerners, have been killed, and more displaced in the conflicts that followed. The civil war ceased in effect with the formal independence of the Republic of South Sudan in 2011, though an echo continues in the north Sudanese region of Darfur.

Sudan is thus another case of religion being used as a rallying point for peoples engaged in a war with non-religious foundations. The Sudanese war is driven by differential development which allowed the north to dominate, and by the presence of key natural resources in the south. The distinction in religions is a factor in the history of development, but probably less so than the inadequacy of roads and railways. Different religions go along with different languages, cultures, and orientations, the south looking to Kenya and Uganda, the north to Egypt and the Arabian peninsula: this is not, however, fundamentally a conflict between Muslim and Christian. The south is quite possibly not even a Christian majority country: statistics are not reliable, but indigenous tribal religions may predominate, whilst Islam is a significant minority.

Moreover in Darfur, north of the border, resistance to Khartoum is spearheaded by the Justice and Equality Movement, whose very name signals secular concerns. It is devoted to the empowerment of local ethnic groups that straddle the borders of Sudan and Chad. But its founder, Khalil Ibrahim, was previously a supporter of Hassan al-Turabi, one of the key figures in the Islamization of Sudan.

Religious loyalties have doubtless helped individuals reconcile themselves to fighting, and motivated groups to remain loyal to the whole. But religious feeling is not what divided Sudan. The divisions had secular roots, which happened to map, very roughly, onto religious differences.

Nigeria

A similar story can be told of the Biafra war in Nigeria (1967–70). Nigeria, though constitutionally united, is an alliance of historically very distinct groups. The three main ethnic groups, Hausa, Yoruba, and Igbo, make up around two-thirds of the population. The Hausa, occupying more northerly territories, became predominantly Muslim by contact with North Africa; Yoruba and Igbo came under the influence of seaborne Christian missionaries.

We have seen (p. 27) how in recent centuries religious purification movements established distinctive Muslim polities; one of these was the Sokoto caliphate, which came into existence in the early 19th century, and some of whose institutions passed into the British imperial system and thus into independent Nigeria after

1960. Sokoto was in fact a creation of the Fulani people, a smaller group within what is now Nigeria, and early adopters of Islam, who have since then become somewhat intermingled with the Hausa. This pre-existing unity allowed the Hausa and Fulani to dominate the early years of Nigeria.

The tension between north and south was sharpened by the presence of large oil deposits in the coastal regions. Just as in Sudan, a northern, predominantly Muslim area was politically more unified and powerful, but the natural resources were in the south. In 1967 Emeka Ojukwu, an Igbo chief and military governor of Nigeria's eastern region, led a secessionist movement with the aim of a mostly Igbo state of Biafra. The rhetoric of the Biafrans was explicitly Christian. Biafra described itself as an embattled Christian nation, menaced by a jihad. This distinction became sharper as foreign Christian organizations brought aid to Biafra, and apocalyptic millenarianism became more and more popular in the embattled and suffering region. But again, this was a war fought for predominantly ethnic, economic, and political reasons, rather than in pursuit of religious goals.

Sri Lanka: an artificial rivalry?

In May 2009, as the battle between Sri Lankan government forces and the Liberation Tigers of Tamil Elam (LTTE or 'Tamil Tigers') was reaching its climax, the normally muted United Nations spoke of a bloodbath in northern Sri Lanka: the Sri Lankan government protested the phrase. This was the end of a civil war which had gone on at least since 1983 and arguably since 1975. The final phase of the war alone displaced nearly 300,000 people and left perhaps as many as 40,000 dead in an island with a population of little more than 20 million.

The roots of this conflict are deep, complex, and disputed. Three-quarters of the population have Sinhalese as their first language; most are Buddhist, though some adhere to other religions, and there are small but influential Christian communities. Besides a small Muslim minority, the remainder are Tamil-speakers, mostly Hindus. A minority within Sri Lanka, this group has strong ties with the Tamil-speaking population of the Indian state of Tamil Nadu, less than 100 km away across the Palk Strait. The population of Tamil Nadu is nearly 70 million, that of India over 1.3 billion. Two-thirds of Sri Lankan Tamils trace a long ancestry in the island; one-third descend from workers brought in during colonial times.

Pre-colonial structures of governance lent themselves to coexistence. Buddhism had grown up within Hinduism and, particularly in southern India and Sri Lanka, the two had much in common. Moreover, pre-colonial polity emphasized conformity of practice, not conformity of belief. The king was the centre, around whom orbited groups and individuals who could have different beliefs and attitudes so long as they joined in shared rituals. But from the middle of the second millennium, a new way of thinking came on the scene: the outlook of European colonialists. It gave the Portuguese, the Dutch, and finally the British a technological edge which let them take control of Sri Lanka.

By applying this way of thinking to the web of Sri Lankan life, however, the colonial powers sharpened the contrasts between religious identities. Britain wrote into the 1815 Kandyan Convention, which consolidated its hold on the island, a responsibility to protect the 'Religion of the Boodhas'. This provision may have been motivated by a desire to protect a religious minority within the empire. But it also had the effect of drawing a hard distinction between Hindu and Buddhist which would later become a focus for animosity.

This distinction hardened after independence in 1948. Acts of Parliament removed citizenship from Tamils not descended from long-established native communities. A proposal to make

Sinhalese the country's only official language sparked anti-Tamil rioting. Parliament made further laws seen as disadvantaging Tamils in the years that followed. In the 1970s resistance turned to a military struggle. Whilst this certainly was a conflict between Hindus and Buddhists, it was no clash of religions of the sort we have seen in the crusades. The fundamental motivations to fight were political. Many of the laws that focused the conflict after independence were promoted as a way of building a majority behind a governing party. Many Sinhalese perceived a threat posed by India to the north.

Buddhism was a factor: but it was an act to promote the Sinhalese language, rather than to enshrine 'the Religion of the Boodhas', which was the watershed. Moreover S. W. R. D. Bandaranaike (1899–1959), who first proposed this law, though Sinhalese, was from a long-established family of Anglican Christians. A small community of Sinhalese Anglicans had been relied on by the British government in India to administer Ceylon since the early 19th century. Sirimavo Bandaranaike (1916–2000), his widow, who succeeded him as Prime Minister and finally instituted the law, was descended from Kandyan Buddhist aristocracy, but educated in a Christian convent.

Sri Lanka was thus a conflict in which religion provided a focus of unity to each side, in a war that had more generally political roots. But it is particularly interesting to notice that the points of conflict between these two religions had themselves been sharpened by the impact of a third religion from outside.

Conclusion: faith or flag?

In all these examples we have seen how religion can be implicated in war even if it is not the primary motivation. It can be a boundary marker. It can provide a uniting myth—and in so doing can itself be re-forged. It can provide solace and purpose for individual combatants and a rallying cry for communities and nations. Yet it may do all these things without being the main reason why the war is fought.

It is worth noting that the examples in this chapter have usually been of later date than the examples in Chapter 2. This suggests a general world-historical trend toward the de-coupling of religion and politics. Of course, there is nothing inevitable about this trend. It may swing back the other way in the next 2,000 years—if we survive that long. But certainly, between the days of the divinity of the Roman emperor and today something has changed. Partly, religion has become more universal. Christianity and Islam both have pretensions to being true everywhere and for everyone. This is a contrast with the particular and local religions which were far more dominant 2,000 years ago, in which gods were often understood as no more, and no less, than the gods of a particular tribe or nation.

Two thousand years ago there were many societies in which it made no sense to distinguish between religious and political structures. The emperor was a god. Government and war were forms of worship, dependent for success on divine favour. Today it is quite understood that nations at war with one another may yet have a religion in common. We saw in Chapters 1 and 2 that Christianity was very much bound up in the passions and symbols of the First World War, for good and for ill. At the same time, most of the combatant nations were Christian in character, often with a national Church, but a Church in some sense a branch of a worldwide Christian fellowship. The Church with the greatest claim to universality, the Roman Catholic Church, was also one of the strongest voices against hostilities.

This makes it harder today than in the past to distinguish between holy wars and wars fought for secular purposes under religious flags. The religious element in the wars of the United States, both externally and in the American Civil War (1861–5), will always be

9. Paul Henry Wood, *Absolution Under Fire* (1891), depicts an actual event during the three-day battle of Gettysburg in Pennyslvania (2 July 1863): the Jesuit priest Father William Corby, from the University of Notre Dame, stands on a boulder, 'exhorting the soldiers' (probably from the Irish Brigade) 'to remember the noble cause and sacred nature of their duty', encouraging them 'to make a sincere act of contrition before receiving conditional absolution'.

particularly hard to pin down. The Civil War engaged religious feeling and symbols on both sides, and certainly the anti-slavery movement which bolstered the resolve of the North had deep roots in Evangelical Christianity. The divisions in the American Civil War were to some degree theological divisions, with each side offering a radically different interpretation of what God was doing in the war, and of the legitimacy of slavery. Both Catholic and Protestant religious leaders preached about the war, with priests and pastors accompanying and encouraging the troops of both sides (see e.g. Figure 9). But it was also a clash of economic systems, and a clash of constitutional ideals: agricultural and slave-owning against industrial and capitalist; confederation versus union. Likewise, many of America's external wars have been called, by friend and foe alike, 'crusades', whereas they have actually been motivated by other things: freedom, and oil, to give two non-religious examples.

An intriguing argument has even been made that war has itself taken on a religious quality in America. The argument is that the particular form of religion that was central to the foundation of the United States was a form of Protestantism in which salvation could be readily conceived of as a matter between the individual and God alone. Thus the element of collective loyalty, necessary to enact a common purpose in a new nation, had to come from somewhere else. In the hundred years that followed, this common purpose was forged to a degree in war, and it was Christian sentiment and imagery which made this possible. The Congregationalist Minister Horace Bushnell (1802–76) wrote in 1863 of fighting in the Civil War as 'a political worship, offering to seal itself by martyrdom in the field'.

This is a story that poses some really difficult analytical challenges. But these challenges will always arise when we consider war and religion. No one paradigm will explain all situations. We will always need to think hard in order to come to a view of whether a war belongs in Chapter 2, or in Chapter 3: whether it is a holy war, fought for religious purposes; or a secular war made possible by religion which provides symbols around which populations rally, and passions to stiffen the sinews of the soldiers at the front.

Chapter 4
Mitigating the horrors of war

The Commander-in-Chief of the British army is also the Supreme Governor of the Church of England. Priests accompany British regiments into battle, their involvement formalized since 1796 through the Army Chaplains' Department. The 1982 Falklands (Malvinas) conflict ended with the raising of the Union Flag, combining the cross of St George with the cross of St Andrew, and a telex from the British commander confirming the Argentine surrender which signed off 'God save the Queen'. Religion is of course less central to the life of the British army today than in past centuries, and the religious pluralism of wider society is reflected within its ranks. But religion remains woven into its fabric, as it is to a greater or lesser degree in the warp and weft of other armies, from the United States to Iran. And one must then ask, what kind of influence that is.

Does religion mitigate the violence of the British army, or provide a focus for belligerent energies, or a cloak of moral respectability? Does religion, as we saw in the case of First World War shrines, by making suffering and sacrifice more bearable, allow war to be prolonged beyond what could otherwise be endured? If it mitigates fighting, making it more humane and less terrible, does it also give it greater legitimacy? Religion may reduce the harms of war: but if by doing so it makes it easier for a nation to fight with a clean conscience, this may be a more subtle form of assistance that religion renders to those who want to prosecute wars for their own purposes.

We need to have this tension at the back of our minds as we turn now to situations in which religion, rather than motivating or assisting war, has sought to be a force making warfare *less* barbarous and catastrophic.

The *Mahabharata* and the moral tensions of war

Many religions have a distinctive ethical code with regard to war. The Western Christian tradition has developed a concept of 'just war', and the Islamic notion of jihad also places limits on war. But perhaps the oldest body of ideas and teachings on this topic arose on the Indian sub-continent. This thought receives a subtle treatment in the *Mahabharata* epic. Composed over several centuries and put in final form around the 5th century, describing events supposed to have occurred many hundreds or thousands of years earlier, the *Mahabharata* is the story of the dynastic struggle between two rival families, the Kauravas and the Pandavas. The latter are represented by five warrior brothers, the eldest of whom, Yudhishthira, is the rightful king. The climax is the immense Battle of Kurukshetra, which leaves only the Pandavas standing. Dismayed by the terrible slaughter they renounce the world and, clad in rags, make their way into the Himalayas toward heaven. The characters in the book are to a degree deified, and though the action is set in the material world, the story has a strong mythic flavour.

The ethical core of the epic is the conflict between different forms of *dharma* (roughly speaking 'duty'). *Kshatriya-dharma*, which we have met with in Chapter 2, is the duty of the *Kshatriya*, the warrior or ruling class; the ethical code proper to warriors. Besides prohibiting retreat, and specifying that an honourable fight is one between equals, it also puts limits on war, restricting where a blow may be struck, and prescribing that non-combatants should not be killed. *Raja-dharma* is the code by which kings are meant to rule: its focus is security and order. Intermingling with these two is the concept of *apad-dharma*, the duty proper to times of chaos and warfare, when some forms of underhand behaviour and violence may become acceptable.

The Pandava brothers, the heroes of the saga, are warriors and kings, and they fight and rule in a time of great crisis. Thus they are answerable to all three of these codes. In the crucible of the Battle of Kurukshetra, the tensions between the codes are laid bare. In battle the Pandavas repeatedly transgress the limitations imposed by the *kshatriya-dharma*, because as kings they are driven by the imperative of the *raja-dharma* to preserve their rule. Some of the subtlest discussion comes in the section of Book 6 of the *Mahabharata* known as the *Bhagavad Gita* ('song of God'). This contains a long dialogue between Arjuna, one of the Pandava brothers, and his divine charioteer, Krishna, an avatar of Vishnu (Figure 10). Arjuna has grave doubts about the fight and experiences a conflict between his duty as a warrior to fight and the ideal of non-violence (*ahimsa*) espoused by the renouncer traditions. He falls into despair and lays down his weapons. Krishna reminds him of his duty as a *Kshatriya* to fight for a righteous cause. As the text unfolds Krishna resolves Arjuna's doubts and gradually reveals himself as supreme Lord, the creator, maintainer, and destroyer of the universe.

The role of Krishna is ambiguous: he counsels a morally balanced approach to warfare, yet does not use divine power to prevent the catastrophe. Warfare emerges as an unavoidable reality of human life, and as a space that is morally grey. In war, balances have to be struck between different moral imperatives: courage, order, compassion. A key insight comes when Krishna advises Arjuna that he need not desire the fruits of victory, nor to be killed, nor even to kill, since the consequences of his fighting, even life or death, are not the ultimate reality:

10. Scene from the *Mahabharata*, showing Arjuna riding out to battle with Krishna as his charioteer. Arjuna's dialogue with Krishna in the *Bhagavad Gita*, part of the epic, is central to the development of Hindu thought on the ethics of war. This scene, and the epic of which it is part, has been represented in Indian art and culture for thousands of years, including two popular big budget Indian TV adaptations of the Mahabharat, in 1988–1990 and more recently in 2013, in which Bollywood star Shaheer Sheikh portrayed Arjuna.

who wealth and power do most desire

Least fixity of soul have such...

...Let right deeds be

Thy motive, not the fruit which comes from them.

And live in action!...

Unto pure devotion

Devote thyself: with perfect meditation

Comes perfect act, and the right-hearted rise—

More certainly because they seek no gain—

Forth from the bands of body, step by step,

To highest seats of bliss...

This is an ethic of detachment only in the sense that the material outcome of the war is less important than how and why you fight or do not fight. But if it is a detached ethic, it is by no means an ethic of renunciation. On the contrary. The *Mahabharata* has been convincingly read as a Hindu riposte to the growth of Buddhist ethical teaching. The founder of Buddhism, Siddhartha Gautama, was, like the mythical Pandava brothers, a member of the warrior caste, who renounced this role to become a spiritual guide. Two centuries later, Buddhism had been adopted by the Indian king, Ashoka (*c*.265–236 or 273–232 BCE). Ashoka had begun his reign using force to consolidate his empire, but, dismayed by its horrors, sought to renounce the ethical compromises inherent in war. It seems likely that the Hindu thinkers and writers who finalized the *Mahabharata* epic used it in part as a riposte to this way of thinking. The mythical king, Yudhishthira, by contrast with Ashoka, fully inhabits the moral conflicts that are the lot of kings.

The *Mahabharata* thus presents an understanding of the ethics of warfare in which compromise is unavoidable. In the crucible of war, there is no simple right answer. This rich and subtle ethic of war fighting is pithily summed up in the much criticized 2000 military courtroom drama *Rules of Engagement* (director William Friedkin), in which Colonel Terry Childers, on trial for excessive use of force, asks rhetorically, 'You think there's a script for fighting a war without pissing somebody off?' The answer which the *Mahabharata* gives, with a hard-won profundity, is 'indeed not'. Whether this ethic mitigates the harms of war is a challenging historical judgement beyond the scope of this book. It undeniably offers morally committed soldiers a framework for the hard work of trying to fight the least bad war.

Islamic military jurisprudence

We saw in Chapter 2 that the Muslim tradition, even if elements in it have sometimes provided the motive force for fighting, also

offers detailed ethical resources for mitigating the harms of war.
They have their roots in the Qur'ān, and in the collections of
sayings and deeds of the Prophet. From these roots different
schools of thought have grown up. The main distinction is
between Sunni and Shi'a thought, though even within these two
branches there are numerous sub-branches and controversies. As
in any other large body of thought, there are many different
approaches.

The core of the Islamic approach to war and peace, as to many
other matters, is the practice of juridical reading or 'Shari'a
reasoning'. This practice became necessary when early Muslims
found themselves governing large tracts of territory and thus
needed to derive a body of general law from the fundamental
texts. Different interpretations arose and by the 8th century
different schools of jurisprudence could be distinguished. As every
major book on Islamic law from the classical period includes a
treatise on jihad there is a wealth of thought on the topic. It is not
a monolithic body and there is scope for internal disagreement,
but three themes recur frequently: rule, restraint, and reciprocity,
and we shall consider each of these in turn. We also need to
become more familiar with the practice of Shari'a reasoning, by
which these concepts have been developed and by which, where
they conflict, they are reconciled. As we shall see, the importance
of this practice has been reasserted in recent decades of instability.

Rule. War is an evil in Islam, but there is little foundation for the
notion that it is an absolute evil to be shunned whatever the
consequences. This may lend credibility to an Islamic ethic of war.
Even a liberal modernist interpreter of the Islamic tradition can
say with confidence that Islamic law 'does not require Muslim
jihadists to love their enemies nor to receive them with damask
roses'. What the Muslim must do, however, is strike a balance. War
has a religious basis, but it is still an evil: 'Fighting has been
prescribed for you, though it is hateful to you' (2.216). To be just a
war must thus have a religious basis. And if war is a religious

activity, it is subject to the rule of religion. Islam may prescribe war, but it also prescribes with equal authority the rules by which war is to be fought.

A classical statement of this position is in the 'Book of Foundations', a key text of the early and highly influential Muslim jurist Muhammad al-Shaybani (*c.*750–805).

> Whenever God's Messenger sent forth an army...He said: Fight in the name of God and in the path of God. Fight the mukaffirun [ingrates, unbelievers]. Do not cheat or commit treachery, and do not mutilate anyone or kill children. Whenever you meet the mushrikun [idolaters], invite them to accept Islam. If they do...let them alone...If they refuse, then call upon them to pay tribute. If they do, accept and leave them alone...

Islam makes adherence to law a central component of religious observance, so an ethic of war that begins 'Fight in the name of God and in the path of God' is committed to war within legal limits, subject to rule. First and foremost there must be a proper authority for war. This sense of fighting in the path of God was strengthened after the death of the Prophet. The young Muslim community asserted that it honoured Muhammad but, in honouring him, served God. God's Prophet had sent forth armies to fight in the path of God. Now his successors would do the same.

This is why the Muslim ethic of war condemns brigands, who by definition fight without the authority of the Muslim community. There is leniency for bona fide rebels who take a stand against authority on the basis of the Qur'ān. But 'As for bandits and those who slay without a ta'wil [a religious interpretation], irrespective of whether they are a group or individuals, they are to be slain...' The requirement for a legitimate, ultimately divine, authority for war is at the heart of some of the most significant controversies of the present day, as we shall see.

It is not, however, the only element in the Muslim commitment to rule-bound warfare. Treaties are also taken very seriously. Treachery is frowned on, even against non-Muslim enemies. Pledges of safe-conduct once given must not be withdrawn. Non-Muslims who submit to Muslim rule when conquered are protected by rules, though in most interpretations they enjoy this protection only if they themselves obey the rules.

A fascinating insight into the interplay between ethics and rules comes in a discussion reported by al-Shaybani, who asks Abu Hanifa, whose disciple he was, what would be the legal treatment of a Muslim who received a pledge of safe-keeping from a non-Muslim ruler, went into that ruler's territory, and under the protection of the pledge killed and robbed and brought his booty home. Abu Hanifa answers that there is no punishment for this man, because he did these acts outside the jurisdiction of Islam. But then, 'I asked: would you disapprove of [the Muslim's] committing such acts? He replied: Yes, on the ground of his religion, I disapprove of his dealing treacherously with them.' He has acted wrongly; but he has not contravened the rules of war.

Restraint. At a greater level of detail there is then a large body of law that restrains the conduct of war. This again descends from sayings and actions attributed to the Prophet. We saw earlier how al-Shaybani, in the tradition with which he begins his *Book of Foundations*, recalls that the Prophet forbade mutilation, or the killing of children. From this and similar sources developed detailed doctrines placing restraints on what may or may not be done in war. Combatants must not be summarily executed or tortured; the wounded must not be put to death; captives must not be burned, nor corpses mutilated.

It is also important to distinguish combatants from civilians. The latter usually include children under 15, women, old men, monks, peasants, merchants, diplomats, and the sick. There is room for debate: some jurists consider all monks to be non-combatants;

others take them to be non-combatants to the extent that they conduct themselves harmlessly. But anyone falling into the category of civilian must not be killed or injured, and their property must not be destroyed. This principle also leads most jurists to put considerable limits on the use of indiscriminate weapons, particularly fire and inundation. On the other hand some jurists accept that such weapons may sometimes be used and that in such cases the unintended killing of civilians is permitted.

Another set of rules restrains the wanton harm or destruction of resources. Religious, medical, or cultural buildings may not be destroyed. Important elements in the economy are safeguarded: Ibn Qudama, for example, considers the treatment of bees, concluding that they may not be drowned, and that most authorities forbid the burning of hives. There is also a general prohibition of rape, ethnic cleansing, and massacres.

Reciprocity. The third fundamental intuition in Islamic military jurisprudence is the principle of reciprocity. The following passage from the Qur'ān typifies this theme, which occurs in several other places:

> And if thou fearest treachery from a people, withdraw from them in a just way. Truly God loves not the treacherous... And prepare for them what you can of strength [of arms] and horses tethered [for battle], frightening thereby the enemy of God... And if they incline toward peace, incline thou toward it and trust in God. (8.58–61)

The Muslim may be implacable in a just battle against those who are implacable, but must offer peace to those willing to make peace. Classical Islamic jurisprudence even goes so far as to prohibit attacking an enemy without being attacked first.

Shari'a reasoning. These three ideas of rule, restraint, and reciprocity are not exhaustive, but they cover a good deal of the territory. It is important, though, to be aware that they emerge from a complex web of debate and reflection over many centuries, with a strong juridical character. Most debates in the Sunni tradition are found in legal texts and handbooks. This long legal tradition of individual scholars reflecting on war and the ethics of war is firmly embedded in various Islamic traditions. It is also important to remember that, even where clear principles emerge, they are not separate spheres: they interact, and sometimes conflict.

A historically important example of this interaction is an episode in the rule of Harun al Rashid, the 8th-century Abbassid Caliph of Baghdad. Harun asked scholars to advise whether he could withdraw a pledge of clemency given to a rebel leader, as the leader in question had returned to his rebellious ways. Some advised yes, and some no. In the end he decided to withdraw his clemency. But the jurists who have become normative, and who continued to be held in honour, Abu Yusuf (d. 798) and al-Shaybani (d. 804), argued that Harun could respond to force with force, but was otherwise bound by his pledge. The opposing view, which won out, was that the pledge of clemency was given on the presumption that the leader would behave in a certain way, and was voided when he did not so behave. Here we see 'rule' in tension with 'reciprocity'. In the short term 'reciprocity' determined the outcome. In the long term the consensus was in favour of 'rule'.

This process of negotiation of conflicting interpretations is central to the practice of Islam in the historical perspective. This practice, the practice of 'Shari'a reasoning', is a subtle and complex web of thought-practices developed over centuries by many different practitioners. It is particularly important for the non-Muslim to make an effort to grasp this, because the process of reasoning is not the same as that with which the secular citizen of a Western democracy will be familiar.

Shari'a reasoning starts from two sets of texts: the Qur'ān itself, and the hadith. It is axiomatic that the hadith do not contradict the Qur'ān, but they may help to interpret it. The Qur'ān, in turn, establishes the authority of the hadith. An early practitioner of Shari'a reasoning, al-Shafi'i, developed on this basis the principle of abrogation: if there is a conflict between texts, the later are taken to be normative, though a text from the hadith cannot abrogate one from the Qur'ān. Within this framework, jurists apply texts to resolve questions of ethics and politics in the situations through which they live. Many of these situations have to do with warfare, and about a quarter of the Qur'ān contains relevant material.

This all forms part of a continuing debate, premised on the unchanging letter of the foundational text, but allowing freedom for interpretative energy. It is this which allows Muslims to disagree strenuously with one another, but yet not doubt one another's Islamic commitment. What it is particularly important to grasp is that there is, in the 21st century, an honest attempt to arrive at moral and political positions which are nothing more, and nothing less, than interpretations of the Qur'ān and the hadith. For the reader today steeped in the culture of secular rational modernity this may be such an alien way of thinking that she or he may not grasp what is going on without an imaginative effort.

Emergency situations and asymmetrical warfare. Whilst Shari'a reasoning has been going on for 1,400 years, in the last century or so two important developments have had a big impact on how it works in practice and given it a renewed prominence: the decline of the Ottoman Empire, and the increase in literacy.

The Ottoman Empire, with its centre at Constantinople (modern-day Istanbul), had been weakening and contracting since its high point in the 16th century, when it included tracts of Christian central Europe and laid siege to Vienna. But for all this time a Muslim caliph had ruled over Muslim territories, and over the holy places of Islam. In 1922, having found himself on the losing side in the First World War, the last Ottoman sultan left

Turkey, and in 1924 the caliphate came to a formal end. For the first time since Muhammad, there was no central source of rule whose claims were widely recognized in the Muslim world.

This posed a serious problem for the Islamic ethic of war. War must only be waged by rule, under proper authority. So what happens when the proper authority is no more?

Many answers were offered. And these points of view proliferated because in the last hundred years the numbers of Muslims who can read, and who have access to the fundamental texts, increased dramatically. More and more Muslims engage, formally or informally, in the very Shari'a reasoning which has shaped the Islamic ethic of war over fourteen centuries. And this reasoning, happening in a more fragmented world, has had a broad scope and has grappled with a wide range of unfamiliar situations. Several important and influential new ideas have become prominent. Here we concentrate on just one aspect of this development.

War in the 20th century tended to become less regular. The wars of the Ottoman Empire involved armies under established authority fighting pitched battles. There was little of the asymmetric warfare we know today, which as we have seen is potentially problematic in Islam, with its prohibition on warlike bands without authority. Guerrilla warfare in the 20th century has covered a wide territory, but it has called for a particular explanation when carried on by Muslims.

The key to understanding the Islamic practice of irregular warfare is perhaps the notion of an 'emergency situation'. An established authority is essential for a just war; but this is only because the authority is given the mandate to wage war by God. Many Muslims who oppose the state of Israel look on its establishment as in many ways the continuation of the crusades, the key difference being that there is now no central Islamic authority to sanction resistance. In such an emergency, jihad becomes a duty for all Muslims, and the mandate to wage war can be received by individuals and groups.

There are precedents for such cases in the classical texts. It is Shari'a reasoning of this kind that lies behind the statement in the Hamas 'Document of General Principles and Policies' that 'Resisting the occupation with all means and methods is a legitimate right guaranteed by divine laws…' Armed resistance is envisaged as of primary importance. It is of course possible for Muslims and non-Muslims alike to disagree with the conclusions of the Hamas Charter, and also the reasoning on which it is based. But we need to notice that the reasoning is part of a continuous project of Shari'a reasoning, drawing on the same sources and principles as in past centuries. This constant thread of religious commitment, expressed in a distinctive way of thinking about war, distinguishes the irregular warfare of Muslim groups from that of, for example, the Viet Cong or the IRA. A full understanding of conflicts in which such groups are involved must thus include insights into the detail of the religious commitments of the participants.

Just war in the Christian tradition

Both Islam and Hinduism start from the position that warfare is, if evil, then permissible and perhaps sometimes a duty. Christianity, as we will see in Chapter 5, was for its first 300 years essentially a pacifist faith. When it became the state religion of the Roman Empire, Christianity had to reconcile pacifist doctrines with imperial power. Different ways were found to justify waging war, using, or abusing, Christian principles. By making war permissible, they also set boundaries on it.

The Eastern Orthodox tradition largely remained closer to the original pacifist outlook—it is instructive, for instance, that the crusades were a largely Western endeavour. The Roman Catholic

Church, however, through engagement with the practical and ethical issues of warfare, developed doctrines which have had a broad impact not just on the conduct of religious wars, but on secular thought and international law. Unsurprisingly there are many points in common with the Muslim and even the Hindu outlook. The key principles of this 'just war doctrine' are that a Christian nation may fight if it goes to war for the right reasons (*jus ad bello*, justice in going to war) and if it fights in the right way (*jus in bello*, justice in war). Within these two categories, different thinkers see different sub-headings. Typically for there to be *jus ad bello*:

1. the war should have a **just cause**—national self-defence, protection of the weak and so on
2. it should have **legal authority**—fighting on the authority of a legitimate state or international body
3. there should be a **right intention**—the just cause should not be a flag of convenience for pursuing some selfish end
4. war must be the **last resort**—negotiation, sanctions, etc. must have been tried
5. there must be a **good chance of winning** and thus achieving the just cause
6. it must be a **proportional response**—so that it is highly doubtful that a nuclear war could be just

If these criteria are met and the war begins, then to be a just war it must be fought with *jus in bello*, which typically means:

7. the **harm done must be minimized and proportionate** to the threat faced—for example, enemy soldiers should be imprisoned, not killed, if possible
8. **fighting must be discriminating**—certain targets (hospitals, for example) must not be attacked and non-combatants must be respected.

Just war theory is very influential in the modern world, and closely intertwined with international law on war. The reasons for this are rooted in history. The high point of just war theory as the arbiter of whether and how wars should be fought was the late Middle Ages in Western Europe. Since then just war theory has continued to evolve and is regularly reconfigured and interrogated. For example, scholars such as Lisa Cahill now argue that the traditional divide between just war theory and pacifism, justifying or avoiding war, should be transformed by 'practical and hopeful interreligious peacebuilding'. Though never a single political entity since the Roman Empire, Europe was highly unified, and wars were fought under the authority and direction of the Church. Many bloody wars were fought, but the history of the *Pax Dei* (see p. 32) suggests that their harms were to a degree mitigated.

After the Reformation, however, the Church could no longer claim to be a central regulator of war. To fill this vacuum, Protestants began to develop what has grown, over many centuries and drawing on different traditions, into the body of international law governing warfare. Those who set this project going did so with the materials to hand. Principal among these was the doctrine of just war. Today, international law has a strong focus on the individual through a concern for human rights. But ideas like just cause, proportionality, and lawful authority are still important elements in the justification and control of war by bodies such as the United Nations.

Many Christians continue to reject the compromises inherent in just war theory. One of the most compelling is Stanley Hauerwas, an influential American theologian, who argues that just war theory is not simply wrong, but internally incoherent. Just war theory is not 'compatible with realism'. He says that since Constantine 'realists' have said that Christians confronted by military evil cannot simply surrender and allow themselves, or other innocents, to be killed or enslaved; order and peace must be preserved by war against the threat of war. Hauerwas, however, thinks this impulse to 'realism', once it establishes that *some* war is acceptable, will press the Christian to accept *any* kind of war. If fighting is realistic, civilian deaths, torture, and the bombing of hospitals are also realistic as the price of victory. In the terms in which we posed the question at the start of this chapter, this line of argument says that where religion seeks to mitigate the harms of war, it always ends up justifying and prolonging it.

Engagement and moderation: peaceful religious groups in warring nations

So far we have seen how the religious perspective of a nation has, in different ways in history, offered resources for making warfare more humane and less destructive. Recent centuries, however, have seen a proliferation of denominations and sects within unitary nations—within nations that have themselves lost much of their religious character. These different groups offer different outlooks on war and peace. Sometimes they exercise a counterweight to militarism from within.

At the personal level a striking illustration is provided by Corporal Desmond Doss, an American infantry medic in the Second World War. His story was told in the 2016 film *Hacksaw Ridge* (director Mel Gibson). Doss was a pacifist, motivated by his commitment to Seventh Day Adventist Christianity. Nevertheless he felt compelled to serve in the army. He rejected all forms of violence but won the Medal of Honor for his courage in saving the lives of dozens of his comrades under heavy fire (see Figure 11). American Seventh Day Adventists likewise contributed to the Cold War effort in the 1950s, 1960s, and 1970s by offering themselves as subjects for experiments in defence against bacteriological warfare. Adventists, in their values and manner of life, fit well into the pattern of American Protestantism which has been bound up with war-making. Certainly they cannot be faulted in their

11. Corporal Desmond Doss (1919–2006), a US Army Combat Medic who refused to bear a weapon, in accordance with his commitment to his Seventh Day Adventist faith. He is pictured on 12 October 1945 receiving the Medal of Honor, the USA's highest award for gallantry, from President Harry S. Truman (1884–1972), two months after the latter had authorized the nuclear bombardment of Hiroshima and Nagasaki, killing perhaps 200,000 civilians, and bringing the Second World War to an end.

patriotism. Yet the distinctive calling to serve without violence gives a different complexion to conflicts to which they are party.

Many other denominations, formally or informally, exercise such a moderating influence. Methodists have seldom shrunk from proclaiming Christian commitment to peace; yet after the attack on Pearl Harbor in 1941 American Methodist bishops declared war inevitable whilst at the same time condemning its processes. The United Methodist Church in 1972 declared war to be unacceptable as an instrument of foreign policy, but accepted that states could fight to defend against 'unchecked aggression, tyranny and genocide'.

Mormons, though not perhaps fully occupying the mainstream of Christian doctrine, certainly inherit the foundational Christian imperative against violence. The migration of the Mormons to Utah in the 1840s partly resulted from their reluctance to fight to defend themselves against aggression from more traditional Christians, albeit that Mormon communities had from time to time been driven to take up arms. After Utah became a state in 1896, however, the Mormon Church had to negotiate its pacifist leaning with its commitment to the nation of which it was now a full part. In 1942 Mormon leaders took the view that the Church itself must be against war, but that members of the Church who felt a sense of civic duty to serve in war would not be held to be sinful. Mormons in America continue to oppose developments in military technology and to uphold the rights of conscientious objectors, without condemning the nation when it fights.

The Reformed Jewish tradition is another confession in the USA that occupies this middle territory, speaking in eirenic terms from the heart of a nation often involved in war, without ceasing to uphold the nation as a whole. The Union American Hebrew Congregation has expressed support for wars where the safety, security, and survival of innocents are threatened, and for wars of defence against territorial aggression. There is, however, a strong emphasis on the obligation to study particular situations and general principles in depth, to form a view on any particular war on solid foundations, and take an attitude to it consistent with Jewish ethical principles.

These questions are often argued out in detail in committees of the Central Conference of American Rabbis, whose pronouncements gain weight from the seriousness with which they engage with the issues. There is no standard Jewish response to war. However, in opposing particular wars, or aspects of particular wars, Reformed Judaism encourages engaged activism and the building of alliances, both at the level of domestic politics and in international relations. This approach led, for example, to support for the negotiated ceasefire in the Yom Kippur War of 1973.

Making war gentler or more acceptable?

These chapters have adopted the taxonomy of religions as promoting, supporting, mitigating, and preventing war. In this chapter, moving into the territory of just war, considering the nuanced balances denominations have to find when they are committed both to the state and to peace, the taxonomy is harder to defend. What is the broad impact of this middle way? War is a lamentable necessity that must be fought as humanely as possible: does this make wars less frequent and less harmful? Or does it provide a cloak of respectability for war and thus make it more likely to occur?

Any answer to this question will be contentious. And the answer varies depending on the historical context. Field Marshal Montgomery, a prominent British general in the Second World War, reflected, 'You do not get the best from soldiers unless they have a clear conscience in what they do and are confident that it is right...The moral brief must come from the Church.' For hundreds of years generals have valued religion for its impact on

12. An Italian Catholic priest administers Communion to British soldiers in 1917. In the Great War, as in many other wars, Christians, Muslims, Hindus, Jews, and those of many other faiths were often sustained in the most terrible circumstances by their deeply felt religious commitment.

morale (Figure 12). From this perspective, army chaplaincy must, therefore, contribute to military efficiency. Does it also temper warfare? We conclude with the words of Private Reg Lawrence, 3rd South African Infantry, remembering his Great War service:

> Today the Padre preached on the text *Love your enemies* …
> Afterwards the Colonel gave us a little heart-to-heart talk on the
> desirability of remembering that we had bayonets on our rifles and
> using them accordingly.

The padre's eirenic sentiments may in the end have been ignored, and certainly will not have been taken as much to heart as he might have hoped. But the Colonel still felt the need to speak out against them. Did the padre make war more religious, or religion more warlike?

Chapter 5
Invoking peace

Religion can inspire its adherents to fight, binding the nation together and blessing the troops as they march out; where religious frameworks like jihad and just war theory can mitigate the harms of war, this is on the basis that war, if evil, is sometimes a necessary evil. But not all religions have made this bargain. Throughout history some religious people and groups have sought to resist and prevent war altogether. It is to these that we now turn.

As we do so, it will be useful to have some conceptual distinctions in mind. Religious pacifism is a spectrum. For some, peace is an absolute and indivisible value. For others it is one value among many. Some will take the religious imperative to peace as a simple prohibition on fighting. Some will take it as a command to active peace-building, which may even involve the judicious deployment of force. Likewise there are different ways in which religious pacifism is lived out and has an impact. It may demonstrably stop a war. It may bear witness to peace and inspire others to renounce violence. It may foster over centuries a culture in which war is less likely to happen. Or those who renounce war may be overwhelmed and killed and appear to have failed utterly, and yet, in their own terms, succeed in what really mattered: not fighting.

All this has an important impact on how we analyse the data. For there is a paradox in religious pacifism: by renouncing violence, it renounces one of the most obvious ways to get its point across. The pacifist literally cannot fight for peace. How else then, shall she or he contend for it? And what will happen when she or he contends for peace against someone who is willing to take up arms? Pacifists are often, at least in the short term, on the losing side. Victory in the here and now tends to go to the warlike. This is not to say that peace is absent. Peace is a mighty force, the essential condition for the arts, commerce, and societies to flourish. Only, it doesn't make the headlines. Peace is the dog that didn't bark in the night. For this reason it will often be useful to look at smaller situations in greater detail than when we have discussed religious warfare.

Buddhist pacifism

If there is one religion that in the popular culture of the Western world is associated with peace, it is surely Buddhism. As we have seen in our historical survey this is by no means the full story. But there is a strong emphasis on peace in the core of Buddhism. Siddhartha Gautama himself, who came to be known as the Buddha, was born into a noble family, but renounced his heritage precisely because with worldly power came an obligation to punish wrongdoers. The first of the 'Five Precepts' is to abstain from taking life.

An important element in this rejection of violence is that, beyond the care living beings owe one another, the path of violence is the path of corruption and failure. When a soldier fights 'his mind is already low, depraved, misdirected by the thought: "Let these beings be slain"... If others then slay him... he is reborn in the "Battle-Slain Hell". The reasons for fighting are also suspect. Buddhists typically deny the ultimate reality of suffering and loss, so it is simply a bad bargain to cultivate the misdirected and self-destructive habit of mind needed for fighting, in order to defend oneself against something that is not of transcendent importance. The fundamental striving is for liberation characterized by radical equanimity, sometimes characterized in the Chan/Zen/Son traditions as 'discovering one's buddha-nature'. The personal search for radical equanimity, however, can motivate engagement in public and political movements for peace.

An example of an organization that takes this view is the Soka Gakkai movement. Soka Gakkai is explicit about the relationship between inner and outer: its members 'strive to actualize their inherent potential while contributing as empowered global citizens'. Soka Gakkai was set up in Japan in 1930, disbanded by the government during the Second World War, and re-established during the post-war reconstruction. But it has much more ancient roots than this, being founded on the teachings of the 13th-century Japanese Buddhist priest Nichiren (1222–82).

Since the end of the Second World War membership of Soka Gakkai has grown to more than 10 million worldwide. Members commit to the fundamental discipline of chanting *nam-myoho-renge-kyo*, 'homage to the Lotus Sutra'. The Lotus Sutra is a key Mahayana scripture: chanting its name is thought to bring supernatural benefits, and affirms a determination to embrace and manifest Buddha-nature, to be a locus of both inner and outer peace. Some have accused Soka Gakkai of being a religious cult, and others have been concerned by its proactive entry into Japanese electoral politics through its affiliated political party, Komeito. But it has also found broad acceptance, and has a considerable influence on the temper of Japanese society.

In this it is joined by several other similar movements drawing on the Buddhist tradition, some set up in reaction to the Second World War and the nuclear bombardment of Hiroshima and Nagasaki with which it concluded. As well as living out their religion in Japan, many of these movements witness to peace throughout the world. Nipponzan Myohoji, for example, another group inspired by Nichiren, and established in 1917, has built numerous 'peace pagodas' on prominent sites around the world, including New Delhi, Vienna, and London's Battersea Park. The mainstream Japanese Buddhist Federation has also made promotion of peace one of its primary objectives in the wake of the war.

All these movements have grown and flourished in a nation which experienced war at its most intense and destructive. Modern Buddhist pacifism has also manifested in situations of live conflict. Thich Nhat Hanh (b. 1926), a Vietnamese Mahayana Zen Buddhist master, has, since the 1960s, taken a prominent role in advocating for peace, in his own country and abroad, often travelling between the USA and Vietnam, and building alliances across religious divides. He was nominated for the Nobel Peace Prize by Martin Luther King. His advocacy for peace is integrated with his spiritual practice and teaching: again, the emphasis is on the identity between inner and outer peace.

Perhaps the most enduring image of Buddhist anti-war protest and witness is the terrible spectacle of self-immolation. This, however, is not a simple story. Self-immolation has a long history in Buddhist practice, justified in stories of the Buddha's past lives and the lives of those aspiring to Buddha-nature, as a sign of commitment to the path. Bodily sacrifice is part of the Buddhist narrative, realized, occasionally, in actual practice. In the modern age the paradigmatic Vietnamese self-immolation, captured in a famous series of news photographs, is probably that of Thich Quang Duc, a Buddhist monk who set himself on fire in a street in Saigon on 11 June 1963. The focus of his protest, however, was the suppression of Buddhism in favour of Catholicism by the government of South Vietnam, and in this he was followed by a number of other Buddhist monks and nuns.

The immolation of Thich Quang Duc did, however, come to have a considerable impact on the Vietnam War. His example is thought to have inspired several Americans to set themselves on fire in explicit protest against the war. Adrian Mitchell was moved to write a poem, 'Norman Morrison', about one of them, in which he says:

> On November 2nd 1965
> in the multi-coloured multi-minded
> United beautiful States of America
> Norman Morrison set himself on fire
> outside the Pentagon.
> ...
> He did it in Washington where everyone
> could see
> because
> people were being set on fire
> in the dark corners of Vietnam where
> nobody could see

It is impossible to calculate exactly the impact of such an act on the progress of the Vietnam War, but it is undeniable that it was a powerful focus of attention. It is also worth noting that Morrison was himself a Quaker—a member of a Christian sect with a long history of pacifism and witnessing to peace.

Jainism

The impact of the Jaina faith on peace-building, likewise, has been more at the personal rather than the institutional level. Jainism, like Buddhism, grew out of the broadly 'Hindu' milieu of the South Asian sub-continent. There have been Jains in what we now know as India for two and a half millennia. Jainism, with Buddhism, inherits the Sanskrit concept of *ahimsa*, a philosophy that rejects causing harm to living things. Jains are thus vegetarians, and seek in all aspects of their lives to rid themselves of violent tendencies. Jainism was founded by Vardhamana (c.599–527 BCE) who, like Siddhartha, was born into the warrior caste of the *Kshatriyas*, and rejected the role that came with this birth. Jains occupy positions in the traditionally stratified Indian society that do not impose obligations to fight. They are thus exempt from the moral challenges and complexities so subtly explored in the *Bhagavad Gita*, and in Hindu thought generally (see p. 75).

Jains do not sequester themselves, but have historically often been merchants, fully engaged in civil society. The caste system has thus provided a niche within Indian society in which, through the ebb and flow of war on the sub-continent over 2,500 years, a small but visible minority have witnessed to the ideal of non-violence.

Mahatma Gandhi

One of the names in the 20th century most associated with the hope of peace is that of Mohandas Karamchand Gandhi (1869–1948), known as Mahatma Gandhi, 'Mahatma' being a title of respect meaning something like 'venerable, great souled'. Gandhi was born in India, trained as a lawyer in England, and practised in South Africa where he developed techniques of non-violent civil disobedience. His idea was to forge a method of mass protest to overcome evil by refusing to cooperate with it: to compel the oppressors to conform to their better nature. In practical terms it consisted of concerted actions from strikes, through marches of witness, fasts, and mass disobedience to authority, always without violence.

Whether or not Gandhi was precisely a religious figure is open to debate. He was brought up in a Hindu family, but in early adulthood his keen engagement with Hindu texts was inspired by involvement, whilst in London, with the Theosophical Society, an organization with an interest in Eastern philosophy and spirituality, founded by a Russian émigré in the United States. Gandhi had Muslim friends and acknowledged the influence of Jainism, as well as the example of Jesus Christ. In a European or Middle Eastern context, this kind of spiritual eclecticism could be a sign of a secular outlook. In India, where religion is typically more capacious, welcoming, and open-ended, and less credal, than further west, it is probably more accurate to see it as a further iteration of an ancient tradition, adept at drawing in imagery and ideas from beyond.

Gandhi's Indian movement, which he started to develop after a long apprenticeship in South Africa, was rooted in the culture of the continent it sought to liberate. Gandhi, who had formerly dressed as an English lawyer, adopted the simple robe and loincloth of the Indian holy man, drawing on 3,000 years of religious culture to focus hearts and minds on peace. However one labels Gandhi's religious outlook—he was certainly committed to religious pluralism—*ahimsa*, the Hindu concept of non-violent respect for all life, taken up by Jains and Buddhists, was an important part of it. And again, in drawing on this ancient concept rooted in the soil of the land, he focused long-established religious commitment in the cause of peace.

Bacha Khan

Spy magazine, an American satirical magazine that flourished in the 1980s, once published a chart of the World Championship of War, showing progress to the semi-finals, setting up a forthcoming final between two unseeded outsiders who each beat one of the favourites in the semi-final. The first, Vietnam, knocked out France and then the USA; the second, who progressed by besting Britain and the Soviet Union, was Afghanistan. Like many good jokes this one contains an important truth. For Afghanistan is, indeed, a warlike country, where fighting qualities are held in high honour, particularly in the culture of the Pashtuns, the dominant ethnic group in that country and the North-West Territories of

Pakistan. Indeed the Taliban, a primarily Pashtun body, appears now to have achieved at least a draw against the combined forces of NATO.

This makes the case of Bacha Khan (1890–1988), the 'frontier Gandhi', all the more striking. Born Abdul Ghaffar Khan in the extreme north-west of British India, he established the Khidmatgar movement in 1929. This organization, literally 'Servants of God', was a non-violent movement of resistance to British rule, and had much in common with the approach favoured by Mahatma Gandhi, of whom Bacha Khan was a close friend (see Figure 13).

The British imperial government tried to suppress the Khidmatgar but without success, and the organization played a

13. Mahatma Gandhi (Mohandas Karamchand Gandhi, 1869–1948), pioneer of non-violence, visits Bacha Khan (Abdul Ghaffar Khan, 1890–1988), a Pashtun who became known as the 'frontier Gandhi', pictured with other members of the non-violent Khidmatgar protest movement, literally 'Servants of God', sometimes also known as the 'Red Shirts' (*Surk Posh*).

significant part in the political pressure that led to independence in 1949. Bacha Khan and the movement he led opposed the partition of India and faced a backlash after the establishment of Pakistan. Through the early decades of Pakistan's existence he continued to advocate for civil rights and the autonomy of the Pashtun territories in Pakistan, keeping to the principles and practices of non-violent civil disobedience.

What is particularly striking about Bacha Khan is that he succeeded in inspiring and leading a movement committed to peaceful resistance that appealed to the broad mass of Pashtun society, a society for whom religion and fighting had long been central values. Perhaps it was only by drawing on the first of these that Bacha Khan could have challenged the second. This hopeful story does not end in peace, however. With the coming of the Soviet Union to Afghanistan the Pashtuns, perhaps understandably, reverted to their martial habits, and the legacy of the 'Frontier Gandhi' was overtaken by the very different religious approach to war adopted by the Mujahideen militias and the Taliban.

The limits of liberal approaches to peace-building

After the end of the Cold War, many in liberal Western countries hoped war could become a thing of the past. What has come to be known as 'liberal peace-building'—in reality many different approaches with a loosely shared ideology—has sought to bring peace to many hotspots around the world. Blue-helmeted soldiers in white four-wheel-drive vehicles bearing the insignia of the United Nations are the most visible manifestation of liberal peace-building, though it also works through diplomacy, development, economics, and many other channels. It is an approach based on problem-solving; it sees its desired outcomes, and the ways to get to them, as universal; it emphasizes institutions, such as democracy and schools; it takes a general view of humanity and works from the top down; it also has a strong theme of economic development. This approach has not been without success. It is striking that the countries of the Warsaw Pact, in effect under Soviet rule for three or four decades, did not descend into civil war when left to their own devices.

But liberal peace-building is not an approach that works everywhere. Its greatest successes have arguably been in countries where attitudes and institutions have been shaped by centuries of Christianity: it has been less successful in places with different religious roots. Critics of the liberal peace-building approach note that, though it acknowledges the power of the local, it simply tries to co-opt it, rather than working with what is particular to places and people. In particular, it tends to see the religious as a generic unknowable 'other'. Though it may try to appropriate local religious sites and symbols, this is done without acknowledging their distinctive power. This approach often runs into difficulty beyond the Western world that gave it birth: for example the challenges and limited success of Western liberal attempts to build peace in Iraq and Afghanistan. The pretensions of secular liberals to articulate a universal truth are hard to stomach in lands where it is easy from a historical point of view to see this as another round in the long cultural struggle between Christendom and the Umma. We explore these issues in greater depth in Chapter 6.

Contemporary Muslim peace-building

Partly in reaction to failures of the liberal peace-building project, there has in recent years been a growth in peace-building initiatives that understand and leverage the peaceful potential of particular religions well beyond the Western liberal comfort zone. This has been a powerful force in countries with strong and dominant Muslim communities. It is impossible to generalize. In the so-called 'Muslim world' one size certainly does not fit all, for Islam, like all great religions, is plural. Thus these efforts involve drawing both on local tradition and on Qur'ānic sources, and recognize the importance of individual religious leaders. Peace, and those who advocate for it, needs legitimacy, justification, and cultural rootedness. The very idea of what peace is, and how one is to talk about it, varies from place to place. These insights are all at odds with the liberal project; but approaches that build on them have succeeded where liberal peace-building has struggled to make inroads.

Dekha Ibrahim Abdi (1964–2011) was the founder of the Wajir Peace and Development Committee, an influential federation of organizations in northern Kenya (see Figure 14). She pioneered the use of traditional Somali practices of mediation and negotiation, combined with Qur'ānic authority. She and the organizations she has inspired and built have also offered hospitality for interfaith dialogue. Muhammad Tahir-ul-Qadri (b. 1951), a Pakistani imam and leader of Minhaj-ul-Quran International, issued a 600-page fatwa condemning all forms of suicide bombing. It drew on extensive Qur'ānic scholarship,

14. **Dekha Ibrahim Abdi (1964–2011), peace activist and organizer of Somali ethnicity based in Mombasa, Kenya, who pioneered the use of traditional Somali practices of mediation and negotiation, combined with Islamic principles, to build peace and promote interfaith dialogue.**

making the case against violence without presupposing norms beyond those most Muslims would respect.

These two very different examples show common principles at work. The starting point is not a generalized notion of global peace and universal human rights, but the grounded commitments of a particular faith community, within a well-established culture. Thus the effort at peace-building has something solid on which it can gain traction. Moreover there is often a focus on a single individual with a personal authority, around whom a group can come together to take action.

Critically, Islamic theology and practice offers in both cases a frame of reference for inter-communal discussion. Peace can be treated not as an absolute value but as the side-effect of commitment to deeply shared values of justice and mercy. This is very important. In making the case for peace it is vital to recognize what is held in common, taken for granted, and what is not. In the Western world, significantly shaped by its Christian history, the concept of peace as an absolute value is well understood (notwithstanding that Christians have fought many wars). It may, thus, work as a starting point.

While there are many different forms of effective peacekeeping (see e.g. Figure 15), robust peacemaking, and creative peace-building, this may also help to explain why certain forms of liberal peace-building appear often to be less successful beyond the historical boundaries of Christendom. Different cultures, shaped by different religious traditions and cultural expectations, have different notions of peace, and value it in different ways. The Islamic understanding of peace is, in the most general terms, less a matter of the simple absence of war, and more a matter of forging a stable and secure community under God. Thus the simple refusal to fight is less likely to feature in Muslim pacifism than in perhaps Buddhist, Christian, or secular liberal approaches.

15. United Nations peacekeepers join Kathy Calvin, CEO UN Foundation, left, and Executive Director of UN Women, and former President of Chile, Michelle Bachelet after visiting a Peace Hut, a forum for community justice, in rural Liberia, Monday, 7 March, 2011. Ms Bachelet and Ms Calvin are visiting Liberia to commemorate the 100th anniversary of International Women's Day, 8 March.

Without entering deeply into the religious outlook that has shaped the culture of a given place, it is going to be hard, perhaps impossible, to mobilize the resources needed for a lasting peace. If this level of engagement is absent, if it leaves no space for individuals and institutions forged in the particular religious culture of a place, the liberal peace-building may not succeed. It risks being seen as an external imposition and paradoxically becoming a form of peace that can only be enforced by violence. Perhaps lasting peace will only be brought to Afghanistan by a new Bacha Khan.

Pre-Constantinian Christianity

We have seen how Christians have justified violence, how Christian nations have fought terrible wars, and how Christianity has been as destructive of peace as any other religion, and more so than many. But peace remains for Christians a central value with very deep roots.

Although the Hebrew Bible, the Old Testament of Christianity, offers justifications for war, there is almost nothing in the New Testament that works this way. On the other hand themes and phrases like 'love your enemies' (Matthew 5: 44/Luke 6: 27/Luke 6: 35) and 'put away your sword' (Matt. 26: 52/John 18: 11) recur frequently. Perhaps most significant is the conduct of Jesus himself. The contemporary expectation of a Messiah was that he would be a mighty military leader who would expel the Romans from Israel. A Messiah who rode into Jerusalem not in a chariot but on a donkey (Matt. 21: 7, John 12: 14), and submitted to execution without protest, offered a very different narrative.

No significant Christian thinker of the first two or three centuries countenanced violence. Tertullian (*c*.155–*c*.220), one of the most combative of early Christian theologians, took 'love your enemies' to be the 'principal precept' of the ethic of Jesus. Origen (*c*.185–*c*.255) argued against Christians fighting for the Roman Empire, saying, 'God did not deem it in keeping with such laws as his…to allow the killing of any individual.' There are few if any definitive records of Christians serving in the Roman army until the end of the 2nd century.

The picture is not clear cut: soldiers are often portrayed positively in the New Testament, and Christians were reluctant to serve in the army because soldiers had to participate in mystery cults. But Christians of the first two or three centuries were solidly against fighting. During this time Christianity grew from a minor sect of Judaism to an organized faith with adherents across the empire, an important tier of civil society, administering charity and offering community to outcasts.

What impact did this large, articulate body of Christian pacifists have on the warlike tendencies of the Roman Empire? It is hard to say they had any at all. Orthodox Roman citizens criticized them as free-riders: 'if all were to do the same as you...the affairs of the earth would fall into the hands of the wildest and most lawless barbarians'. The Roman Empire continued to wage war more or less continually. If the early Christians sought to shape the politics of the empire it was through appealing to the higher nature of violent leaders, exposing and condemning wickedness.

Christians only started to shape the empire after the Emperor Constantine himself became a Christian. In the decades that followed, as Christianity became the established religion of the empire, new approaches to violence emerged in the Christian community. By the middle of the 4th century, Christians distinguished between murder, which continued to be prohibited, and killing in war, which could be permitted. As we have seen (pp. 69–72) this was the period when the Western Church began to articulate what has come to be known as just war doctrine. By the 5th century Christians were highly influential in the conduct of imperial policy; but they were by the same token no longer a pacifist Church.

Christian pacifism since Constantine

Since that era Christianity has, in different ways, continued to a greater or lesser degree to be integrated into states that have fought wars. From century to century, however, sects and movements have broken out from the institutional Church and reverted to the earlier pacifism.

The Eastern Orthodox Church, though not wholly pacifist, resisted the concept of holy war. This may have rendered the Eastern Roman Empire less militarily efficient, and contributed to its decline and fall. In the West, every few centuries saw a revival of interest in the fundamentals of Christian faith, and a renewed interest in the pacifism of the early Christians. This often found expression in monastic renewal: Benedictines, then Cistercians, then Franciscans all turned their backs on worldly concerns, from riches to war. As we saw on p. 64, Muslim just war theory usually protects monks from harm in war, reflecting a respect for this renunciation of violence. Monks in turn mitigated the harms of wars by offering healing and hospitality. Few monks, however, fought: the monastic order that got most directly involved in the politics of war was the Knights Templar who for all their piety were no pacifists.

In the mid-second millennium Western Christianity fragmented. Many of the new Churches made an accommodation with armed force, but some returned to the pacifist instincts of the early Church, particularly those Churches that came to be called Anabaptists. One of their founders, Menno Simons (1496–1561), preached on loving enemies, turning the other cheek, and beating swords into ploughshares. Statesmen of the 16th century often saw Anabaptist communities as a threat to good order, and many were destroyed; but Mennonites have continued through five centuries as a fundamentally pacifist Church, whose members may not fight in wars. The Quakers were another among many such pacifist Christian sects—as we saw above, a Quaker, Norman Morrison, was among those who immolated themselves to protest against the Vietnam War.

Kaduna

The last thirty years have seen a resurgence in tensions between religions, sometimes bursting out in warfare. This has called forth a response in the form of initiatives to promote interfaith dialogue and understanding. One example is the Interfaith Mediation Centre based in Kaduna, in northern Nigeria.

Kaduna is the capital of Kaduna state, which straddles the hazy but strongly felt boundary between the predominantly Muslim north of Nigeria, and the predominantly Christian south. The IMC was set up by a Muslim imam and a Christian pastor, Dr Muhammad Ashafa and Dr James Wuye, both Kaduna residents, in response to inter-communal violence in 1992. The centre promotes dialogue and understanding between religious leaders, trying to articulate the peace imperative in the scriptures of both Islam and Christianity. One of its most imaginative initiatives is to leverage the network of mosques and churches in the area to provide a form of early warning system so that nascent inter-religious violence can be spotted early and defused.

The IMC also articulates a counter-narrative to the idea that northern Nigerian conflicts are fundamentally religious. The IMC's argument is that violence results mostly from economic and climatic changes, which has driven northerners further south as the Sahara desert has expanded, where they have competed with established communities over scarce land and water. Where these conflicts have turned violent, they have often done so under a religious banner, because this is the pre-existing cultural dividing line between the two groups. But the roots of the conflict are not religious. In short, the violence in northern Nigeria belongs in Chapter 3 of this book, not Chapter 2. In offering this counter-narrative the IMC seeks to take the heat out of the situation, and make a space for the peaceful elements of both religions to have an impact.

Conclusion

Whether one is optimistic or pessimistic about religious pacifism depends to a degree on one's perspective. In the short term, pacifists are often, for obvious reasons, on the losing side. In the softening of human manners, in the growth of organizations like the Red Cross, Red Crescent, and Red Magen David, we may see a slow filtering of religious pacifism into the mainstream, but from century to century we keep on fighting wars. For many, the greatest power of religious pacifism, however, is seen only in the perspective of eternity. Stanley Hauerwas acknowledges that pacifism is often not, in the short term, the practical and effective option; but he thinks religious people—Christians, at least, for whom alone he would presume to speak—are called to the impractical. This hold on the eternal may be what enables religious pacifism to persist down the centuries in the face of recurring warfare. Religious pacifism is often less interested in effectiveness than in faithful witness. Ironically this may over the longer term make it a highly effective force for change, but it will often work under the radar, individual pacifists having an impact through influence and example over generations.

Religious peace-building is often not a news event, but the absence of a news event. It is not the high drama of a crusading army on the march. It is an imam and a pastor drinking tea together week after week—the result of which, often enough, is that nothing noticeable happens. And that nothing noticeable happening is one kind of peace.

Chapter 6
Questioning religion and war

If you have a chance to visit Jerusalem, take some time to consider religion and war from a suitable vantage point in the Old City. In the air around you, you will hear the bells of the Church of the Holy Sepulchre, the call to prayer from half a dozen mosques, and perhaps the sound of an extended Jewish family playing music and singing as they bring a child to the Western Wall for Bar or Bat Mitzvah.

Then ascend above the crowded, tunnel-like streets of the Souk and look for the Temple Mount and the Haram esh-Sharif (Figure 16). If you can see one you will see the other, for they are the same, highly contested space. The Temple Mount is the site of a series of structures, culminating in Herod the Great's Temple, which was destroyed by the Romans in 70 CE. The Haram esh-Sharif ('Noble Sanctuary') is, for Muslims, the location of the Prophet's Night Journey, and the third holiest site in Islam. Not strictly a holy place for them, this space is of keen interest to Christians too, since Jesus walked, prayed, and taught here: and this was one reason the crusaders came.

Jews, who have fought wars of determined ferocity for millennia over this particular piece of land which the God of the universe gave them. Muslims whose Prophet was himself a warrior, who are called to jihad, who conquered and brought peace and order to

95

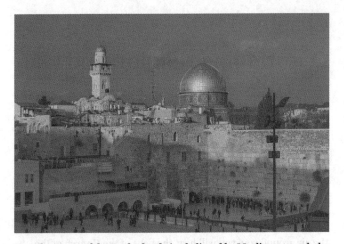

16. The Dome of the Rock, the shrine believed by Muslims to mark the
site from which the Prophet began his Night Journey to heaven. The
third most holy place in Islam, it is built at the centre of what was
formerly known—and continues to be known by some—as the Temple
Mount and by others as Haram esh-Sharif. In the foreground can be
seen the Western Wall which, being the only part of the original
structure still readily accessible, has become an important place of
Jewish prayer. It is also believed by Muslims to be near to where
Muhammad tied his steed.

this place in the name of their universal faith. Christians, who
believe God came from the realm of the infinite into this world to
renounce violence, but who themselves visited this place with
apocalyptic fury in the crusades. Each faith has a profound,
complex, and distinctive relationship to war and peace.

Note, too, that of all world religions, these three have perhaps
most in common. They have a shared inheritance of overlapping
texts, language, place, and architecture. As you sit in your corner
of the Souk, Japanese and Chinese tourists will pass by, some
doubtless Buddhist, some practitioners of Shinto, others perhaps
Confucians. Think how Muslims, Jews, and Christians may look to
them: branches of the same, alien tree.

It takes a real imaginative effort to enter into the mindset of someone who adheres to a different religion or belief system from our own. This is true if you adhere to a religious tradition of great antiquity, or if you belong to that fast-growing sect who put their faith in No Religion. And the challenge is an order of magnitude greater if we seek also to enter into the outlook and experience of someone from centuries past. Imagine going on pilgrimage to Roman Jerusalem shortly after the legalization of Christianity in the 4th century. Temples to the old gods of the empire are still being demolished. Eastward in the desert tribal polytheism flourishes, as yet unchallenged by the Prophet Muhammad. Visit again in the 11th or 12th centuries at the height of the great clash between Christendom and the Umma: stand on the walls looking out, or on the hillside looking up, at the alien and warlike face of your implacable enemy with whom you share scriptures and an unshakeable belief in the one God of Abraham, Isaac, and Jacob, in a world where the very idea of atheism is unknown.

After four chapters in which we have done little but tell stories and ask questions, you may be hungry for overarching theory. To what extent does religion predispose its followers to war or to peace? What is the fundamental relationship between war and religion? In this chapter we shall probe how far one can go in seeking such general conclusions. We shall press this enquiry quite hard. We may not, however, be able to take it as far as the tidy-minded would ideally wish. And the reason for this is bound up with the unfathomable richness and variety of life you have seen and imagined, from the stone bench where you sat sipping mint tea in the half light of the Suq el Qatanin.

Concepts and categories

If we seek general conclusions about war and religion, it may help to become familiar with some of the framing concepts offered by the study of religion. If we come up with conceptual categories that make sense of the history, that may tell us something about 'religion and war in general'. If we fail in the attempt, that may tell us something else.

One influential, and highly generalizable, notion of religion is that of the German philosopher of religion Rudolf Otto (1869–1937). Otto taught that the core of religion, what is common to all religions, is 'the holy'. The holy might be described as a human experience of something beyond human experience. This experience of the holy is powerful, and, when we are in its grip, we are both drawn to it by its immensity and beauty, and daunted by its scale and implacability. The fusion of these two qualities gives rise to the 'numinous consciousness' which Otto held to be the central feature of religion.

The sociologist Max Weber offers a different, but likewise highly generalizable concept of what religion is. For Weber, religion is a system of meaning or symbols central to the functioning of a society. Religion here is something substantive, expressed in particular ways and making particular claims on its adherents; but it can be fully analysed by the sociologist.

Both these approaches think of the core of religion as being something abstract, something which drives the actions of its adherents, and to which these actions point. An alternative approach is to ask, for example, 'How does this particular religious person actually live? What rituals does he or she join in, and how? What is it like to live in this way?' This approach identifies religion as primarily something that is lived out. Understanding religion in this way tends to put the focus on the individual or the informal community, rather than on the institution and the stated theology. It is not a question of what people *should* think, do, or feel in order to be consistent with the historic, published statements of religion; it is about how they actually *do* think, act, and feel.

Thus in very general conceptual terms, we can distinguish two very broad groups of approaches to religion. The first might for example be called a 'credal' or 'substantive' approach. The second might be described as 'functional' or perhaps as a matter of 'lived religion'. Within each of these groups there is room for a good deal of nuance. But there is an important distinction between theories of religion that focus on the core notions, experience, or belief; and those which start with instances of how communities of faith live.

In 'credal' terms, perhaps the most heavily freighted distinction that is often drawn *between* religions is between monotheisms and other religions. The key feature of monotheisms is that there is only one God, who is universal, infinite, and eternal. It has often been observed that over the last 2,000 years monotheism has very much increased in dominance, with the growth of Christianity and Islam, and some commentators have seen in this a natural progress or development towards a more universal outlook.

Distinguishing monotheisms is, however, harder to sustain if you take a 'lived religions' approach. For example there are some striking similarities between some of the devotional practices of Hindus and Christians. They have different theological rationales, but the veneration of particular saints in a Warsaw church may look and feel quite similar to the worship of particular gods in a Madurai temple, and very different from what happens in a Riyadh mosque.

Besides these general concepts for thinking about religion, it is also possible to make some general observations about developments in religion and war in recent years. From 1945 to 1989, war and politics was dominated by the tension between two world views, embodied by the USA and the USSR. Then, to the surprise of many, the Cold War ended—not least because the Afghan Mujahideen defeated the Red Army. Moreover, the postmodernist outlook, with its rejection of grand narrative, was also gaining popularity in the Western world. Thus many who sought an overarching story within which to live their lives turned more and more to religion, and sometimes to particularly fundamentalist forms of belief.

At the same time many of the states founded as colonial empires were struggling to hold together. Common purpose was hard to find, and many suffered from inherited poverty and corruption. Cold War superpowers had propped up authoritarian regimes which weakened after 1989. When the hard edges of dictatorship wore thin, other forms of loyalty, older and more deeply felt, re-emerged. They were often religious.

This period also saw increased movement of people around the globe. This has had two contrasting impacts. It has led some people to identify less with those beside whom they live than with those with whom they share religion and culture. It has also encouraged the strengthening of religion as a marker of local, national identity, conferring 'in-group' status, in a reaction against globalization.

All these trends have combined in recent decades to bring religion back into the foreground, giving it again a power in international affairs which it has in fact almost always possessed through the broad sweep of history.

Does religion make for war?

There are indeed, then, general terms in which we can try to think of religion and war. The aim of speaking in these terms is to see if we can draw broad conclusions about the big questions. As in many fields of academic enquiry, there is some merit in searching for propositions that may be generally true, that can begin to make sense of a wide range of circumstances, and offer a single answer to a question that arises again and again in different situations. As we have seen, in relation to religion and war, the question that keeps coming up, and which many take to matter the most, is whether or not religion in general does, or does not, tend to cause and intensify war in general.

Strong arguments are put forward on both sides. If you think religion makes for war, you may start by saying that religion makes claims about ultimate values. Thus religious people tend to think the ends justify the means: war may even be an evil, but not as bad as defying God's purposes. And however terrible war may seem in the here and now, religious people may say that the sorrows of war are balanced by a reality beyond the material world. As we have seen, some religions can energize their followers to fight with fearless ferocity, sure in the hope of an eternal reward.

If on the other hand you think religion makes for peace you may start from the observation that religion is concerned with a search for the good, and strives to broaden connectedness among human beings. Religious concern with the ultimate and universal prompts us to look beyond the interests of our own tribe or nation to the needs of others. Moreover, religious people are subject to the judgement of God, who is concerned with order and good. And true religion helps its adherents endure the risks of refusing to fight, sure in the knowledge that thus they tread the path of eternity.

Those who take this positive view of their religion or religion more generally, where they see it implicated in warfare (as in the crusades, or as a motive for terrorism) will argue that religion has here been misunderstood or misappropriated.

There is another view, a subset of the first, which we must note briefly. It is that religion is *uniquely* warlike, that the history of war is the history of religion, and that the best way to reduce or eliminate war is to supplant religion with a secular outlook. This view has gained a good deal of publicity through the articulate advocacy of 'New Atheists' such as Richard Dawkins and

Christopher Hitchens. An alternative perspective is to be found in William Cavanaugh's *Myth of Religious Violence,* and *Fields of Blood* by Karen Armstrong, which makes the detailed historical case that religion is not in itself distinctively and uniquely warlike.

Perhaps the most compelling evidence in this strand of the argument is the middle years of the 20th century. Organized religion had but a minor role in the Second World War and the conflicts surrounding it. It is hard to say that secular warfare was gentler or less destructive than the religious variety.

Another strong general conclusion that we might seek to draw is that there is something distinctively warlike about monotheistic religion. It is certainly true that star billing in Chapter 2 went to Christianity and Islam. Both are committed to a God who is explicitly the God of everything, everywhere. It is hard to say that this commitment did not contribute to the energy with which adherents of these two closely related faiths fought territorial wars in the late first and early second millennium.

Against this argument we could notice that Judaism, historically perhaps the most influential of monotheisms, doesn't fit the pattern. Judaism has often been warlike. But the motivation to fight does not come from universalism. The God of Judaism is indeed the God of all. But of the Jewish people he demands particular things, and to them he makes promises, in particular the promise of a land, for which they have often fought. It is these particularities, rather than the universality of God, which are arguably involved in Jewish religious warfare.

Another problem with the theory of warlike monotheisms is that our examples are a biased sample. Freddie Mercury, lead singer of Queen, was born Farrokh Bulsara, in a Parsi family. Parsis practise the Zoroastrian faith, perhaps the oldest monotheism, exalting Ahura Mazda, the 'Wise Lord', creator of all. In 2001 there were about 70,000 Parsis in India, and a similar number in the rest of the world. Why are they known as Parsis? Because their forebears were exiles from Persia. For a thousand years Zoroastrianism shaped the culture and way of life of a vast empire in and around modern-day Iran until in the 7th century both religion and empire were struck down by a new and more militarily efficient monotheism: Islam. Perhaps, then, monotheism is not inherently warlike, but the monotheisms we know best are those that happened to win wars. Christianity and Islam do have a history of warlike conquest, but this may say less about the link between monotheism and war than about the link between war and power.

There is a strong case both for and against the idea that religion in general drives war. The New Atheist argument that religion is *uniquely* warlike is hard to sustain. It is not clear that monotheisms have a particularly strong tendency to fight. What can we hope to say that is broadly true?

One influential and stimulating approach to this question is that of Scott Appleby. He sums up his attempt to grapple with the question whether religion is or is not inherently warlike in the phrase 'the ambivalence of the sacred', which he expands in an influential book of the same name. Appleby draws on the idea of 'the holy' we met earlier, the central concept in Rudolf Otto's understanding of religion. Appleby uses the term 'the sacred' interchangeably with 'the holy'. He defines religion as 'the human response to a reality perceived as sacred'. Because of the great power of the experience of the holy/sacred, this response can be very powerful. Because this response is a human response, it can take many different forms.

This is not to presuppose anything about the nature (or existence) of God. God may be peaceful, yet our holy/sacred experience may come into lives that are not peaceful, and our encounter with the holy/sacred may move us to violence. This could be an authentically religious response, even if in some theoretical, theological sense erroneous. Appleby's key point is that in the human experience of that which is beyond the human, there is both power and ambiguity. Thus authentic religion has great power both for war and for peace.

Appleby's approach does seem to offer to say something generally true about the relationship between war and religion. He does not, however, claim to resolve the question whether religion does or does not make for war.

What does this ambiguity tell us about the question?

Religion is inherently warlike. Religion is inherently peaceful. Religion incubates under its ambivalent wings the possibility of both war and peace. What do you think? This book is not meant to get you off the hook of forming your own opinions by a diligent weighing of facts and concepts, but rather to furnish you with history, concepts, and insights with which to work.

In that spirit let us challenge you to take one further step back, to look at the scene in a broader perspective. We have found no consensus on the question whether religion in general is or is not warlike in general. And this, you might think, is strange. For the materials needed to form such a judgement are not hard to find. This is not an obscure question about the nature of life at the bottom of the Marianas trench, or concerning sub-atomic particles without mass or charge. It is a question related to some of the largest and best-documented events and institutions in the history of the world. Can it be, then, that our very failure to reach concrete general conclusions tells us something about the subject?

So leave aside whether religion is warlike or peaceful. Ask a bigger question. A question that should be implicit in all we have been talking about. A question we have to ask unless we are to smuggle a big idea into the debate without any justification at all, which may confuse us deeply. The question is, 'is there any such thing as religion-in-general?' Is there a generic religion-in-general which we can examine to determine whether or not it is warlike?

Turn back to the preceding four chapters. What did we find? In Chapter 2 we saw cases where religion created and inspired terrible wars: through history and across the globe, wars have been fought in pursuit of religious objectives, as the fulfilment of religious duty, and as the expression of a religious way of life. In Chapter 3 we saw situations where religion acted as a flag of convenience for wars fought in pursuit of non-religious objectives, rallying armies and populations to achieve territorial or dynastic goals. In Chapter 4 we saw how religion has softened the terrible harms of war, protecting the innocent and challenging the combatants to restraint. In Chapter 5, we saw religious people and groups steadfastly resisting the temptations and threats of warfare, and becoming, sometimes at great cost, bringers of peace.

In each case something we would want to call religion is involved. In many cases, the *same* religion. The Buddhist Samurai ethic that steeled the nerves of Japanese soldiers in the Second World War is in some respects the same Buddhism that informs the peaceful teaching and practice of the present Dalai Lama. The Christians of pre-Constantinian Rome and Reformation-era Anabaptist communities rejected all forms of warfare, as the expression of a Christian faith no less sincere that that in which the crusaders did deeds of unimaginable violence.

The notion of the 'ambivalence of the sacred' is perhaps the closest one can come to a general statement about the relation between religion and war. But there are two problems: an issue to do with the experience of different religious people, and a more structural issue about the frame of reference in which these questions are considered. We look at these two problems in the next two sections.

The need for a religious perspective

Consider Mohamed Atta and Franz Jägerstätter. Jägerstätter was an Austrian farmer who refused to serve in the German army during the Second World War and was thus executed on 6 July 1943. Mohamed Atta was an Egyptian graduate student and urban planner who piloted the hijacked American Airlines Flight 11, crashing it into the World Trade Center on 11 September 2001. Both men professed themselves to be moved by their religious faith: Jägerstätter was beatified by the Roman Catholic Church in 2007. More recently, film-maker Terrence Malick translated Jägerstätter's story into a film: *A Hidden Life* (2019). To make sense of the idea of religion-in-general it would be necessary to say that both these men were responding to and living out in some ways the same thing. The idea of 'the ambivalence of the sacred' is exactly that: the lives and deaths of Mohamed Atta and Franz Jägerstätter were both authentic responses to the sacred.

There is some power in this idea. Both men faced danger and death with a fortitude many of us would find hard to summon. Something powerful was at work in their lives. Their responses were different in quality, reflecting their own life experience; their responses had a similar magnitude and power, reflecting the holy/sacred core. Perhaps we can think of the holy/sacred as like the process of nuclear fission, which can find expression in a power station or a bomb.

The difference between nuclear fission and the holy/sacred, though, is that nuclear fission is a physical process which we harness as our moral purposes dictate. Whereas both Jägerstätter and Atta, so far as we can know, took it for granted that the holy/sacred, the experience of which drew forth their very different responses, was itself filled with purpose. The holy/sacred is not just power; it is also purpose. The element of value and purpose is central to Rudolf Otto's original idea of 'the holy'. The holy compels us not just because of its fascinating and tremendous might: it has 'a might that has at the same time the supremest *right* to make the highest claim to service...' It has '*objective* value that claims our homage'.

That Jägerstätter and Atta were motivated by something which had for each of them a power of similar magnitude seems at least eminently arguable, if not obvious. But was what compelled them to act similar not just in power but in purpose too? This is what we have to say if we are going to argue they both responded to the same thing. Is this to make the notion of the holy/sacred so elastic that it ceases to be helpful?

Moreover, if we want to make this judgement, we have to recognize that we are claiming to understand something about both Jägerstätter and Atta and their religious experience which they themselves did not know. For it seems very likely that Jägerstätter and Atta would each have thought the other very different from himself. And this is a problem across the whole spectrum of lived religious experience wherever we want to keep hold of the notion of religion-in-general. What do you think? Do you know more about the fundamental nature of religion than a Seventh Day Adventist confined in a military jail for refusing to fire a gun? Or than a Jewish Zealot hurling himself against the ordered and implacable spears of a Roman legion? It is defensible to answer 'yes'. But even if we think we know more about religion than the individual religious person, we have to be careful not to devalue the religious perspective altogether, if for no other reason than because we may thus miss data which can help form a balanced view.

If the 'ambivalence of the sacred' is a call to investigate and enquire into the breadth and variety of religious commitment in the crucible of war, well and good. If it is a way of understanding religion-in-general as one thing, we need to consider carefully whether it is a useful concept. The question is, can we say anything accurate about the nature of religion-in-general, without claiming to know more about it than practitioners of any particular religion know? And are we prepared to do this?

Presuppositions in our ideas of religion and war

If on the other hand we do recognize that we need a religious perspective to understand religion, then that is obviously going to make it harder to come to general conclusions about these questions. They are simply questions it is very hard, perhaps impossible, to stand outside. We seek an objective vantage point, but if we are honest in our enquiries we have to engage with the possibility that an objective perspective may not exist. This brings us to the second problem with making general statements about the relation between religion and war: the structural issue of the frame of reference in which we ask these questions.

We have seen that general conclusions in this field are hard, if not impossible, to formulate. This seemingly negative result, if we press it hard enough, may disclose something interesting. Perhaps our failure is not the result of a contingent lack of effort and imagination, but of something necessary and structural in the nature of the topic. Perhaps if we can't reach a general conclusion about war and religion, we may learn from our failure something worth knowing about the debate and how it is framed.

Reverse the telescope. What does our search for religion-in-general tell us about the context in which we search? Go back to some of the things religion-in-general, might be: we drew the distinction between substantive/credal notions of religion, and the functional/'lived religion' understanding. The first way of understanding religion often leads to describing religion as belief in something: the supernatural, the eternal, the transcendent; or as a shared experience of something beyond: the holy or sacred. And the really interesting distinction between religions in this perspective is that between monotheism and the rest. And even when we come to speak of religion in functional terms, and look at how it is lived, this has often been in terms of how it establishes norms of behaviour through symbolism and shared ritual.

Although specialists in the field may not find it so, the idea that religion is about belief in something infinite that forms our behaviour through shared stories and symbolism will sound uncontentious to many. Even the atheist, who rejects religion, often has this kind of thing in mind as what he or she is rejecting. But it is really a very specific idea of religion. Unsurprisingly it is a general notion of religion that looks a lot like the very particular religion practised in those communities that for the last 500 years or so have been geopolitically dominant. It is a general statement of Western Christianity, particularly its Protestant variety.

This is not a novel observation. Identifying our received ideas of religion and refusing to buy into them perhaps lies behind some of the most interesting thinking about religion. The 'lived religion' school is among those approaches that insist on the lively plurality of religious forms, which have to be understood to a degree in their own terms. It insists on paying careful attention to the experiences and practices of particular religious people and communities. The 'lived religions' approach is much less likely to describe religion in terms of belief in the supernatural expressed through normative symbols. But the 'lived religions' school is also much less likely to offer a notion of religion-in-general.

There is, thus, a fundamental structural problem with the question about religion and war. It is that our general notions of religion, in terms of which we tackle the question, are really the terms of one particular religion.

Take the 'ambivalence of the sacred'. This was perhaps the most promising approach to thinking about religion in general. But note the terms in which it is stated. Religion is a response to 'the sacred'. 'The sacred' derives from Rudolf Otto's concept of 'the holy'. And Otto stands in a long academic tradition, shaped by Friedrich Schleiermacher a hundred years earlier, of rooting theology in religious feeling. Schleiermacher in turn built on the foundations of his upbringing in Pietism, a Protestant sect that emphasized personal religious experience. All of these deep thinkers did their thinking within the framework of the Enlightenment, itself a reaction against—but also a product of—Western Protestantism. Immanuel Kant, the godfather of the Enlightenment, whose ideas shaped the thought world in which Rudolf Otto lived (and in which we today live), was, like Schleiermacher, brought up a Pietist.

This may go some way to explaining why a concept of religion-in-general is so hard to pin down. Our concepts of religion-in-general are framed by the presuppositions of one religion in particular, the religion of the geopolitically dominant culture of the last four or five hundred years: Western, particularly Protestant, Christianity.

If this be so, then it might also be worth interrogating the other term in our equation. What is war, in general? Typically, to answer this question we distinguish between war and other kinds of violence. This can be controversial: everyone wants to say that *their* violence is war, whilst the other side is doing terrorism or murder. But there is a distinction to be drawn. Most would agree that the armies of Wellington and Napoleon at Waterloo were fighting a war, and that a robber who stabs a passerby for her mobile phone is not. Wars are customarily taken to involve states and armies, which is why pacifism is a political stance: the pacifist is not just rejecting violence, but challenging the policy of the state. When 'war' is used in other contexts it is with a conscious sense of metaphor: the 'war on drugs' was a striking phrase precisely because it clashed with usual notions of war.

Again, this all sounds fairly uncontroversial: violence, with a state and an organized army on one or both sides. But, like the pervading understanding of religion, these ways of thinking about war are specific to a time, a place, and a culture. The nation state in the form we take for granted today only started to develop 500 years ago in Europe during and after the Reformation. A particular religion was central to the identity of nation states as they coalesced: Roman Catholicism and the Protestant and other Churches that descended from or rebelled against it.

Dial back the calendar a further few centuries, to the high point of classical Islam on the eve of the First Crusade. What did 'war' mean here? Was it a matter of armed conflict between states? Probably not. A recurring motif in Islam is the Umma. There have been conflicts between different Muslim polities in the last millennium, but these were not, at least until the modern era, conflicts between nation states. Not only that, but for many Muslims war is both a broader and a more positive concept. Islam has a long-established notion of war which has nothing to do with armies, states, or violence of any kind. This is the greater jihad, the spiritual striving for self-mastery, which we saw in Chapter 2. Jihad is war, in the fullest acceptance of the word, not a mere metaphor as in the 'war on drugs'. But war is not just armies fighting.

For many Christians, and secular people whose thought-world has been partly shaped historically by Christianity, this stretches the concept of war beyond breaking point; whereas for the Muslim the greater and lesser jihads can be two parts of a single concept. This is not to say one of these perspectives is correct and the other mistaken. It is to notice that they are different; and that the one with roots in Christianity is the one that is used in modern discourse about war. If you had found this book on religion and war to be about the relationship between religion and striving after purity and self-mastery, you might have wanted your money back. There are few War Studies doctoral candidates writing theses on purity and self-mastery. But a distinction between the study of armed conflict between states, and the study of spiritual striving for purity and self-mastery, is not written into the structure of the universe. It is a distinction made by a particular culture with its roots in a particular religion, namely Christianity. For many Muslims, who belong to a community of more than 2 billion people, fighting between armies and striving for self-mastery are, by contrast, parts of the same concept. Only, the conceptual categories in which today's academic debate is conducted were not primarily framed in that community.

This is in no way to make a value judgement between Christianity and Islam. If anything, it is to be critical of Christianity, which has smuggled its particular presuppositions into a debate with pretensions to universality. Even those hostile to Christianity recognize that it has shaped, sometimes by violence, the mindset of much of today's world. But the upshot is that the debate over war and religion is rigged. The terms in which it goes on are not universal and neutral. They descend to a disproportionate degree from one particular religion.

If this is true, then the search for general conclusions about war and religion is not going to succeed. Rather, in order to pay due regard to the particularity of different religions we may need to abandon the idea of religion-in-general altogether. This is the logic of the 'lived religions' school, one of the considerable merits of which is that it does not aspire to a generality that is never going to be available in this field.

The ends of war

Now—take one last step back. Grant that there is no such thing as religion-in-general and war-in-general. Grant that most of our general conceptual categories about religion, and about war, have been formed by one particular religion, and are thus not nearly as general as we hoped. If this is how things are, it brings us face to face with one more unspoken presupposition in the war-and-religion debate, which we have to test and challenge.

Those who are hostile to religion often claim it is inherently warlike. Those who favour religion conclude that it is a force for peace or, where it is implicated in war, it has been misunderstood and warped. Those who think religion inspires both war and the pursuit of peace want to promote the latter and discourage the former. Do you notice, however, what these points of view have in common? They have something in common that is so thoroughly taken for granted that we are scarcely aware that it is an idea. But it is an idea. And like any other idea it needs examination and justification. It is the idea that war is bad.

This is not obvious. We have seen, in Chapter 2, times in history when people have thought war was good. War is the crucible in which the virtues are forged, in which courage, skill, love for comrades and tribe are given full expression. War is where we risk all in the cause of God, the highest form of devotion. You may not agree with these ideas: but they are not obviously incoherent, and many peoples in history have lived by them.

Perhaps there *is* something fundamentally bad about war, which is slowly becoming clear to us as a species. Perhaps aversion to war, even a recognition that it is wrong, lies deep within the human condition. There is some support for this idea in evolutionary anthropology. The change in body composition and face shape from the higher apes to *Homo sapiens*—to softer skin, blunter teeth and claws, lower brow-ridges—may have been part of an evolution away from violence. As we got better and better at cooperating in sophisticated ways to hunt, gather, build shelter, and raise children, the success of individuals became bound up with the success of the group. The groups that succeeded were those that weeded out the violent and disruptive. Social and biological evolution thus intertwined, ensuring the success of the gentler ones who remained.

We may hear an echo of this evolution in the words of Vera Brittain. In *Testament of Youth* she writes of being a young woman, unquestioningly patriotic, casually militaristic, at the start of the First World War. But as the war progresses, working as a nurse, seeing her male friends and relations go off to the trenches and come back, if at all, horribly wounded, she begins to perceive a fundamental, universal truth:

> I wish those people who write so glibly about this being a Holy War...could see a case...of mustard gas in its early stages—could see the poor things burnt and blistered all over with great mustard-coloured suppurating blisters, with blind eyes...all sticky and stuck together, and always fighting for breath, with voices a mere whisper, saying that their throats are closing and they are going to choke...and yet people persist in saying that God made the War, when there are such inventions of the Devil about...

No matter how we may think God is marching ahead of our armies, if we are deeply enough immersed in war we will come to know that it is, fundamentally, wrong. Perhaps, then, the presupposition at the heart of our debates on war and religion is, in some way, fundamental, and stands in need of no justification.

On the other hand, Vera Brittain was reflecting on a very large recent war. No matter how pacific we may have evolved to be, time and again we do fight wars. The weeding out of violent individuals laid the foundations for organized violence of a severity unparalleled in the animal kingdom. Some of the most terrible wars have been fought by nations who at home appear to be the acme of refined civilization.

Can we really say, then, that the idea that war is bad needs no justification? Vera Brittain concludes from her own experience that it is just obviously bad, though it was not until the late 1930s that she became a fully-fledged pacifist. But how would Vera Brittain have viewed the matter had she been a Viking or an Attic Greek, in a culture framed by religion that saw war as good and ennobling? Notice, further, that she uses religious terms in her rejection of war. She does not say this is a holy war and holy war is wrong: she says war is unholy and God is not in it. In this she is being quite orthodox, as a woman brought up in the Christian tradition. It is true, and it bears repeating, that Christians have fought as many wars as anyone and more than most. But it is also true, as we saw in Chapter 5, that for 300 years, until its Faustian bargain with Constantine's Rome, Christianity was an almost entirely pacifist faith. Echoes of this pacifism resurface again and again.

This is not to say that Christianity is the only religion that teaches peace. Only that, as we argued above, many of the ideas that underlie much of liberal discourse do largely have their origins in Christianity. One of these ideas is the presupposition that war is undesirable. Neither is it to claim moral superiority for Christianity. Rather the reverse: if the idea that war is bad is a Christian idea, then Christians who fight an unjust war are twice guilty: of fighting, and of perjury.

What we do want to put front and centre in conclusion, though, is that war and peace are religious values. As we have seen, it is fruitless to speak of religion-in-general: different religions are different. They are also internally fragmented and plural. Nevertheless, the value we place on war and peace has to come from somewhere. If we long for peace, that longing must have roots, and open space into which it can grow.

Wars are spectacular, attracting the attention of historians and commentators. They understandably make news at the time they are happening and are often ruminated upon in the decades and centuries that follow. Wars become markers in time, commonly altering the course of local, national, and international history. They are inscribed on landscapes, buildings, and collective memories. As we saw in Chapter 1, images of war are graven in memorials and painted on walls. Wars are reprised in films and plays, novels and poetry. They leave debris and traces for future generations. It takes decades or centuries to heal the wounds of war.

By contrast the formation of the values of peace is a slower process, often hidden, often overlooked. The paths to peace are narrow and winding. Those who tread them, those who work for peace, often go unnoticed. Peace does not come easily. Watching it can be slow and tedious. The role of lived religions in promoting peace is likewise often overlooked. The traces and origins of such peace-building practices are harder to discern. Nevertheless religious actors and communities are integral to peace-building. It is true, shamefully true, that religious people, even those who profess a faith with a commitment to peace at its heart, have fought, do fight, and will fight. But the fundamental intuition that war, whether fought for religious or secular reasons, is wrong: this too has religious roots. We conclude with the words of a pacifist, deeply influenced by Christianity, a mystic, and a former soldier, Leo Tolstoy. In *War and Peace* he describes the experience of Prince Andrei Bolkonsky at the Battle of Austerlitz, lying where he has fallen wounded as he attempts to stem the Russian retreat:

> Above him there was now nothing but the sky—the lofty sky, not clear yet still immeasurably lofty, with grey clouds gliding slowly across it. 'How quiet, peaceful, and solemn; not at all as I ran,' thought Prince Andrei—'not as we ran, shouting and fighting...how differently do those clouds glide across that lofty infinite sky! How was it I did not see that lofty sky before? And how happy I am to have found it at last! Yes! All is vanity, all falsehood, except that infinite sky. There is nothing, nothing, but that. But even it does not exist, there is nothing but quiet and peace. Thank God!...'

Wars have been fought and will be fought for religious reasons. Yet the revolt against war is also a religious impulse. There are forms of religion that can pierce the fog of war, so that in bright light under broad heavens we may forge the reality of peace.

References

Quotations from the Bible are from NRSV Translators (tr. and ed.), *New Revised Standard Version Bible (Anglicized) with Apocrypha* (Oxford: Oxford University Press, 1995).

Quotations from the Qur'ān are from Seyyed Hossein Nasr (ed.), *The Study Quran: A New Translation and Commentary* (New York: HarperCollins, 2015).

References below are to works in the Further reading unless otherwise stated.

Chapter 1: Remembering wars

Article from the *Nevada State Journal* is in Hittman, pp. 265–6; text of the 'Messiah Letter' is at <https://www.pbs.org/weta/thewest/resources/archives/eight/gdmessg.htm>, accessed 19 May 2020—this and variant translations are in Hittman.

Chapter 2: Waging holy wars

Quotations from Sayid Qutb are from *Milestones*, pp. 98–102, 109–10, and 128.

The text of the Arnold Seschaves document is from Giles Constable, *Crusaders and Crusading in the Twelfth Century* (Oxford: Routledge, 2016), p. 100.

Quotations from First World War clergy are from Jenkins, pp. 42–5.

Chapter 3: Sanctifying secular wars

The quotation from Slobodan Milošević is from <https://cmes.arizona.edu/sites/cmes.arizona.edu/files/SLOBODAN%20MILOSEVIC_speech_6_28_89.pdf>, accessed 19 May 2020.

The quotation from Lt Col. Sugimoto Goro is in Palmer-Fernandez, p. 460, citing Brian Victoria, *Zen at War* (New York: Weatherhill, 1997), p. 125.

Horace Bushnell is quoted in Hauerwas, p. 31.

Chapter 4: Mitigating the horrors of war

Passages from the *Bhagavad Gita* are from the translation by Franklin Edgerton, available online at <https://books.google.co.uk/books?id=Y1guGAfGr6UC>, accessed 19 May 2020.

The phrase 'Shari'a reasoning', the quotation from el-Shaybani, and the phrase 'emergency situation', are from Kelsay: the first two from *Arguing the Just War in Islam*, pp. 4 ff., 100–1, the third from *Islam and War*, p. 97.

The reference to jihadists not being required to love their enemies is from Hilmi M. Zawati, 'Theory of War in Islamic and Public International Law', reprinted in Niaz A. Shah (ed.), *Islam and the Law of Armed Conflict* (Cheltenham: Edward Elgar, 2015), p. 281.

The dialogue with Abu Hanifa reported by al-Shaybani, and the injunction to kill bandits (from al-Shafi'i) are in Reichberg and Syse, pp. 353–4, 358.

For the official translation of the Hamas 'Document of General Principles and Policies' see <https://hamas.ps/en/post/678>, accessed 19 May 2020.

The citation from Cahill is from the back cover of *Blessed are the Peacemakers*. See also chapter 10, esp. p. 360.

Discussion of 'realism' and just war is in Hauerwas, pp. 21–37.

The quotation from the United Methodist Church is in Palmer-Fernandez, p. 305.

The quotation from Field Marshal Montgomery is in Michael Snape, *The Royal Army Chaplains' Department 1796–1953* (Woodbridge: Boydell Press, 2008), p. 308.

The Great War reminiscence is from L. Macdonald, *1914–1918: Voices and Images of the Great War* (London: Penguin, 1991), p. 200.

Chapter 5: Invoking peace

The Buddhist teaching against fighting is in Bhikku Bodhi (tr.), *The Connected Discourses of the Buddha* (Boston, Mass.: Wisdom Publications, 2000), p. 1335.

The purposes of Sokka Gakkai are taken from <https://www.sgi.org/snapshot/>, accessed 20 May 2020.

'Norman Morrison' is widely collected, e.g. in Geoffrey Summerfield (ed.), *Worlds* (Harmondsworth: Penguin, 1974), p. 221.

Citations from Tertullian (*Of Patience*, ch. 6) and Origen (*Contra Celsum*, Book III, ch. 7) and the criticism of Christian pacifism, made by Celsus and reported by Origen (*Contra Celsum*, Book VIII, ch. 68), are taken from <https://www.newadvent.org/fathers/>, accessed 20 May 2020.

Chapter 6: Questioning religion and war

'The sacred' is throughout Appleby, *The Ambivalence of the Sacred*; the specific definition of religion is on p. 8.

Citations from Otto are from Rudolf Otto, tr. John Harvey, *The Idea of the Holy* (Oxford: Oxford University Press, 1950) on 'the holy' and 'numinous consciousness' p. 5 and pp. 25 ff., on objective value of the holy, p. 52.

The citation from Vera Brittain is in her *Testament of Youth: An Autobiographical Study of the Years 1900–1925* (Harmondsworth: Penguin, 1994 (1933)), p. 395.

The citation from *War and Peace* is in Book 3, ch. XVI, of the Project Gutenberg edition <http://www.gutenberg.org/files/2600/2600-h/2600-h.htm>, accessed 20 May 2020.

Further reading

The topic of War and Religion is a huge one, of real and burning importance to the lives of billions of people; and it is a topic to which, as we have sought to argue, people will inevitably bring their own experiences, beliefs, and commitments. The *select* bibliography that follows is meant to be both an invitation and starting point for further investigation.

R. Scott Appleby, *The Ambivalence of the Sacred: Religion, Violence and Reconciliation* (Lanham, Md: Rowman and Littlefield, 2000). Explores how religions can both legitimize violence (as 'sacred privilege' or 'duty') and support non-violent conflict resolution (through 'religious peacebuilding'). Appleby considers the ambivalence of the sacred in a wide range of settings, asking 'why and under what conditions do some religious actors choose the path of violence while others seek justice through nonviolent means'.

Karen Armstrong, *Fields of Blood: Religion and the History of Violence* (London: Vintage, 2014). Extensive three-part study that challenges the claim 'that religion has been the cause of all major wars in history'.

Roland H. Bainton, *Christian Attitudes towards War and Peace: A Historical Survey and Critical Re-Evaluation* (Eugene, Ore.: Wipf & Stock, 2008). Concise survey covers from Antiquity to Nuclear Age, first published in 1960.

Nigel Biggar, *In Defence of War* (Oxford: Oxford University Press, 2013). A defence of Christian participation in war and of the just war tradition.

Arnaud Blin, *War and Religion: Europe and the Mediterranean from the First Through the Twenty-First Centuries* (Berkeley: University of California Press, 2019). Blin, a 'historian of war', focuses primarily upon Judaism, Christianity, and Islam (while also briefly discussing Zoroastrianism and Manichaeism). He argues that between the 4th and the late 17th centuries religion was 'the major driver of the wars that took place in Europe and the Greater Middle East', and that 'during that period and in that part of the world', religion 'not only caused and shaped a great number of conflicts but essentially determined how these conflicts were fought'.

Philippe Buc, *Holy War, Martyrdom, and Terror* (Philadelphia: University of Pennsylvania Press, 2015). A controversial but well-argued book making the case that Christianity has given rise to unequalled violence, arising out of its central faith commitments, and mediated through its impact on Enlightenment thought and modernity.

Lisa Sowle Cahill, *Blessed are the Peacemakers: Pacifism, Just War, and Peacebuilding* (Minneapolis: Fortress Press, 2019). Provides a useful critical historical account of the evolving Christian traditions of just war and pacifism, while also promoting the value of interreligious peace-building.

John Calvert, *Sayyid Qutb and the Origins of Radical Islam* (London: C. Hurst & Co., 2010). Traces the evolution of Qutb's thought and understanding of Islam, while placing it within historical, political, and social context.

William T. Cavanaugh, *The Myth of Religious Violence: Secular Ideology and the Roots of Modern Conflict* (New York and Oxford: Oxford University Press, 2009). Challenges the belief that religion promotes violence. By deconstructing the categories of 'religion' and the 'secular', he goes on to argue that the idea of religion as 'non-rational and prone to violence is one of the foundational legitimating myths of Western society'. For Cavanaugh this myth 'is used to legitimate neo-colonial violence against non-Western others, particularly the Muslim world'.

Niall Christie, *The Book of the* Jihad *of 'Ali ibn Tahir al-Sulami (d.1106): Text, Translation and Commentary* (Farnham: Westgate, 2015). A translation of, and commentary on, an early scholarly Islamic text on the philosophy of jihad—a helpful way to engage with the development of the concept.

David Clough and Brian Stiltner, *Faith and Force: A Christian Debate about War* (Washington, DC: Georgetown University Press, 2007). Dialogue and debate between 'a Methodist proponent of pacifism' and 'a Catholic theologian and just war adherent'.

David Cook, *Understanding Jihad*, 2nd edition (Oakland, Calif.: University of California Press, 2015). Demonstrates how jihad 'has a long history and complex set of meanings'. Includes lucid discussions of the origins, evolution, and controversies related to as well as contemporary uses of the term jihad.

Jared Diamond, *Guns, Germs, and Steel: The Fates of Human Societies* (originally published with subtitle: *A Short History of Everybody for the Last 13,000 Years*) (New York: W.W. Norton, 1997). Provides a controversial explanation of 'why Eurasian and North African civilizations have survived and conquered others'. Diamond challenges the theory 'that Eurasian hegemony is due to any form of Eurasian intellectual, moral, or inherent genetic superiority', suggesting instead that 'the gaps in power and technology between human societies originate primarily in environmental differences' and geographical realities.

Reuven Firestone, *Holy War in Judaism: The Fall and Rise of a Controversial Idea* (Oxford: Oxford University Press, 2012). Explores how the idea of 'holy war' effectively disappeared within Judaism for 'almost two thousand years, only to re-emerge with renewed vigour in modern times'. Reuven 'identifies, analyzes, and explains the historical, conceptual, and intellectual processes that revived holy war ideas in modern Judaism', arguing that this ancient concept of divinely sanctioned warring was revived 'in order to fill a pressing contemporary need'.

Reuven Firestone, *Jihad: The Origins of Holy War in Islam* (Oxford: Oxford University Press, 1999). Based upon evidence from the Qur'ān and early Islamic literary sources, Firestone analyses the origins of Islamic holy war, tracing 'its evolution as a response to the changes affecting the new community of Muslims in its transition from ancient Arabian culture to the religious civilization of Islam'.

Marc Gopin, *Holy War, Holy Peace: How Religion Can Bring Peace to the Middle East* (Oxford: Oxford University Press, 2002). Argues that any peace process (such as the Oslo peace accords) that 'fails to take into account the deep religious feelings of Muslim, Jew, and Christian alike is destined to fail'. Outlines both secular and religious methods of peacemaking.

Helen Hardacre, *Shinto: A History* (Oxford: Oxford University Press, 2017). Detailed, comprehensive, and 'magisterial' historical account of Shinto. Includes useful discussions of rituals and state shrines (chapter 13), such as the use of the Yasukuni shrine to memoralize the war dead, and then how Shinto was blamed during the Allied Occupation of Japan (in 1945) for the 'militarism and ultranationalism' that 'led Japan to war' (chapter 14).

Sohail H. Hashmi (ed.), *Just Wars, Holy Wars, and Jihads: Christian, Jewish, and Muslim Encounters and Exchanges*. A series of twenty essays, covering from the rise of Islam to the present day, investigating the interactions between Muslim, Christian, and Jewish ideas about the legitimacy of the use of force.

Stanley Hauerwas, *War and the American Difference: Theological Reflections on Violence and National Identity* (Grand Rapids, Mich.: Baker Academic, 2011). A series of essays by a leading Christian pacifist, including critical accounts of the dominant role of war in the contemporary USA.

Carole Hillenbrand, *The Crusades—Islamic Perspective* (Edinburgh: Edinburgh University Press, 1999). In this ground-breaking book, Hillenbrand draws extensively upon original medieval sources to explore how the crusades and crusaders were perceived by Muslims, as well as 'how the Crusades affected the Muslim world, militarily, culturally, and psychologically'.

Jolyon Mitchell et al. (eds), *Peacebuilding and the Arts* (Palgrave MacMillan, 2020). Explores the relationship between peacebuilding and the arts (Visual Arts, Music, Literature, Film and Theatre/Dance). Includes examples relevant to the complex relations between religion and war.

Michael Hittman, *Wovoka and the Ghost Dance* (Lincoln, Nebr.: University of Nebraska Press, 1990). A valuable resource for understanding the Ghost Dance, with source material to help provide insights to what it may have felt like at the time.

Mack P. Holt, *The French Wars of Religion, 1562–1629*, 2nd edition (Cambridge: Cambridge University Press, 2005). Through a historical narrative, argues that the French civil wars were 'fought primarily over the issue of religion', where each side saw their opponents as like a pollutant that had to be cleansed from the 'body of believers', rather than as holding a 'body of beliefs' that had to be corrected.

Margaret MacMillan, *War: How Conflict Shaped Us* (New York: Random House, 2020). Based on her 2018 Reith lectures, using numerous examples from the Ancient Greeks to contemporary conflict, MacMillan explores why and how we fight, and what war reveals about humanity. She also argues that wars of 'ideology, whether religious or political, are often the cruellest of all because the kingdom of heaven or some form of paradise justifies all this is done in its name'.

Philip Jenkins, *The Great and Holy War: How World War I Changed Religion for Ever* (San Francisco and Oxford: Harper One and Lion, 2014). A vivid account of the role of religions in the First World War. Examples include how religious leaders promoted their own side and soldiers as martyrs, while demonizing the enemy. Jenkins also explores how Abrahamic religions were changed by the war.

Michael K. Jerryson and Mark Juergensmeyer (eds), *Buddhist Warfare* (Oxford: Oxford University Press, 2010). Demonstrates that 'over the past fifteen centuries, Buddhist leaders have sanctioned violence, and even war'. Eight essays discuss 'a variety of Buddhist traditions, from antiquity to the present, and show that Buddhist organizations have used religious images and rhetoric to support military conquest throughout history'. Examines 'Buddhist military action in Tibet, China, Korea, Japan, Mongolia, Sri Lanka, and Thailand', showing that apparently 'pacifist religious traditions' can be 'susceptible' to 'violent tendencies'.

Mark Juergensmeyer, *God at War: A Meditation on Religion and Warfare* (Oxford: Oxford University Press, 2020). 'Based on the author's thirty years of field work interviewing activists involved in religious-related terrorist movements around the world, God at War explains why desperate social conflict leads to images of war, and why invariably God is thought to be engaged in battle'.

Mark Juergensmeyer, *Terror in the Mind of God: The Global Rise of Religious Violence*, 4th edition (Oakland, Calif.: University of California Press, 2017). Through a wide range of international examples and interviews, considers cultures of violence and the logic of religious violence.

Mark Juergensmeyer, Margo Kitts, and Michael Jerryson (eds), *The Oxford Handbook of Religion and Violence* (Oxford: Oxford University Press, 2013). Forty essays offer an overview of religious traditions, patterns, and themes (such as cosmic war, just war, and conflict over sacred ground), as well as theories and analytical approaches related to religion and violence.

Richard W. Kaeuper, *Holy Warriors: The Religious Ideology of Chivalry* (Philadelphia: University of Pennsylvania Press, 2009). Argues that 'while some clerics sanctified violence in defence of the Holy Church, others were sorely troubled by chivalric practices in everyday life. As elite laity, knights had theological ideas of their own. Soundly pious yet independent, knights proclaimed the validity of their bloody profession by selectively appropriating religious ideals.' Some 'sensitive souls worried about the ultimate price of rapine and destruction'.

John Kelsay, *Islam and War: A Study in Comparative Ethics* (Louisville: John Knox Press, 1993). A comparative analysis of Islamic understandings of 'jihad' with Christian understandings of 'just war'.

John Kelsay, *Arguing the Just War in Islam* (Cambridge, Mass.: Harvard University Press, 2007). Drawing on original sources Kelsay considers how Islamic thinkers over many centuries have 'debated the legitimacy of war' and how their writings shed further light on Islamic understandings of jihad.

Corliss Konwiser Slack, with Hugh Bernard Feiss, *Crusade Charters 1138–1270* (Tempe, Ariz.: Center for Medieval and Renaissance Studies, 2001). Original source material for thinking about the motivations of crusaders.

Peter Lehr, *Militant Buddhism: The Rise of Religious Violence in Sri Lanka, Myanmar and Thailand* (London and New York: Palgrave Macmillan, 2019). Provides a 'discussion of militant Buddhism in three leading Theravadin countries. Discusses how 'a notionally non-violent religion explains and defends the recourse to violence'. Argues 'that militancy and (defensive) Buddhist violence is not a novel development or even a "modern distortion of the true religion", but played a role ever since the first Buddhist kingdoms were established'.

Oliver McTernan, *Violence in God's Name: Religion in an Age of Conflict* (London: Darton, Longman and Todd). Argues that 'terror in the name of God' demands that Christian, Muslim, Jewish, Hindu, and Buddhist leaders go beyond mere 'tolerance' to far more 'proactive and rigorous defences of the right of others to believe and act differently'.

Lee Marsden (ed.), *The Ashgate Research Companion to Religion and Conflict Resolution* (Farnham: Ashgate, 2012). A useful set of essays from a wide range of perspectives on different religious traditions (including Islam, Christianity, Judaism, Buddhism, and Hinduism) and conflict or conflict resolution, as well as international relations and peacemaking.

Jolyon Mitchell, *Promoting Peace, Inciting Violence: The Role of Religion and Media* (London and New York: Routledge, 2012). Explores the ambiguous roles of religion and media in both cultivating violence and building peace. Examples analysed include the First World War, the 1980–8 Iran–Iraq War, and the 1994 genocide in Rwanda.

Jolyon Mitchell et al. (eds), *The Blackwell Companion to Religion and Peace* (Oxford: Blackwell, forthcoming 2021).

Ian Morris, *War! What is it Good For? Conflict and the Progress of Civilization from Primates to Robots* (New York: Picador, 2014). Argues controversially that war 'has made the planet peaceful and prosperous'.

Andrew R. Murphy (ed.), *The Blackwell Companion to Religion and Violence* (Oxford: Blackwell, 2011). Series of forty-five interdisciplinary essays that explore the complex relations between religion and violence from a wide range of perspectives. The volume includes discussions of a wide range of traditions, movements, and disciplines, combined with a series of case studies from around the world.

Susan Niditch, *War in the Hebrew Bible: A Study in the Ethics of Violence* (Oxford: Oxford University Press, 1993). Applies 'insights from anthropology, comparative literature, and feminist studies', to analyse a 'range of war ideologies in the Hebrew Bible', 'seeking in each case to discover why and how these views might have made sense to biblical writers, who themselves can be seen to wrestle with the ethics of violence. The study of war thus also illuminates the social and cultural history of Israel.'

Mark Noll, *The Civil War as a Theological Crisis* (Chapel Hill, NC: University of North Carolina Press, 2006). Explores how the American Civil War 'was a major turning point in American religious thought', arguing that there was 'rampant disagreement' both 'about what Scripture taught about slavery' and 'what God was doing in and through the war'.

Oliver O'Donovan, *The Just War Revisited* (Cambridge: Cambridge University Press, 2003). Re-examines 'traditional moral arguments about war' and 'questions of contemporary urgency, including the use of biological and nuclear weapons, military intervention, economic sanctions, and the role of the UN'.

Atalia Omer, R. Scott Appleby, and David Little (eds), *The Oxford Handbook of Religion Conflict, and Peacebuilding* (Oxford: Oxford

University Press, 2015). Interdisciplinary and comprehensive series of essays on religion, conflict, and peace-building. Theoretical reflection combined with multiple case studies makes this a valuable resource and point of reference.

David Onnekink (ed.), *War and Religion after Westphalia, 1648–1713* (London: Routledge, 2009). Range of essays from different perspectives reconsider the relationship between war, foreign policy, and religion during the period 1648 to 1713.

Gabriel Palmer-Fernandez (ed.), *Routledge Encyclopedia of Religion and War* (New York and London: Routledge, 2004). Valuable reference work, which contains a large number of surveys of different historical situations in which war and religion have interacted. It also includes a wealth of material on smaller and often marginalized religions.

Stephen G. Parker and Tom Lawson (eds), *God and War: The Church of England and Armed Conflict in the Twentieth Century* (Farnham: Ashgate, 2012). Provides discussions of issues such as just war, pacifism, obliteration bombing, and nuclear deterrence.

Sayid Qutb, *Milestones* (Delhi: Markazi Maktaba Islami, 1981/2000). An important original source: Qutb's summary of his philosophy, written from prison, and a text very influential on the philosophy of Islamic groups such as the Muslim Brotherhood.

G. Reichberg and H. Sykes (eds), *Religion, War and Ethics* (Cambridge: Cambridge University Press, 2014). An important and extremely useful source book, containing a wealth of key original texts from the scriptures of the major world religions as they bear on questions of war, with helpful commentaries and summary essays.

Jonathan Riley-Smith, *The Crusades: A History* (New Haven: Yale University Press, 2005). Provides a comprehensive and lucid account of the crusading movement from 1074 to 1798. Includes discussion of the 'theology of violence behind the Crusades, the major Crusades, the experience of Crusading, and the Crusaders themselves'.

Kaushik Roy, *Hinduism and the Ethics of Warfare: From Antiquity to the Present* (Cambridge: Cambridge University Press, 2012). Traces the 'effect of Hinduism on the evolution of theories of warfare from the dawn of civilization until the present era'. Takes 'into account the religious traditions that emerged in India (Buddhism and Jainism) as well as the foreign inputs (Christianity and Islam) and how they have shaped the Hindu view of the relationship between warfare, politics, and good governance'.

Jonathan Sacks, *Not in God's Name: Confronting Religious Violence* (London: Hodder and Stoughton, 2015). Investigates the relationship between religion, violence, and war, and explores the role of sibling rivalry in conflict, arguing that religiously motivated violence must also be countered by both the religious and non-religious.

Perry Schmidt-Leukel (ed.), *War and Peace in World Religions* (London: SCM, 2004). Series of useful essays that explore how religion is both 'part of the problem' and 'part of the solution'. Explores war and peace in both Eastern (Hinduism, Buddhism, Chinese) and Abrahamic (Judaism, Christianity, Islam) religions. Discusses 'inter-religious foundations for peace'.

Regina M. Schwartz, *The Curse of Cain: The Violent Legacy of Monotheism* (Chicago: University of Chicago Press, 1997). Argues 'that it is the very concept of monotheism and its jealous demand for exclusive allegiance—to one God, one Land, one Nation or one People' that has contributed to the construction of 'collective identity forged in violence, against the other'.

Desmond Seward, *Monks of War: The Military Religious Orders* (London: Penguin Books, 1972). Considers the origins in the 12th century and the evolving roles of the Templars, the Hospitallers (Knights of Malta), the Teutonic Knights, and the Knights of the Spanish and Portuguese orders. Explores how these 'noblemen vowed to poverty, chastity and obedience' lived a monastic life while at the same time 'waging war on the enemies of the Cross'.

Larry Siedentop, *Inventing the Individual* (London: Allen Lane, 2014). A broad historical perspective on the shaping of secular liberal moral intuitions in Europe and the wider world through the impact of Christianity.

Michael Snape, *God and the British Soldier: Religion and the British Army in the First and Second World War* (Abingdon and New York: Routledge, 2005). Argues that 'religion provided a key component of military morale and national identity in both the First and Second World Wars', and also that 'Britain's popular religious culture emerged intact and even strengthened as a result of the army's experiences of war'.

Brian Daizen Victoria, *Zen at War*, 2nd edition (London: Rowman and Littlefield Publishers, 2006). Controversially explores the role of Zen Buddhism in supporting (and far more rarely opposing) Japanese militarism through the Second World War. Considers 'the roots of Zen militarism' and 'explores the potentially volatile mix of religion and war'.

Jay Winter, *Sites of Mourning, Sites of Memory: The Great War in European Cultural History* (Cambridge: Cambridge University Press, 1995). A detailed and illuminating cultural history of how the Great War was remembered through memorials, as well as art, films, and novels.

Publisher's acknowledgements

We are grateful for permission to include the following copyright material in this book:

Extract from 'Norman Morrison' by Adrian Mitchell, reproduced with permission of United Agents of behalf of The Estate of Adrian Mitchell.

The publisher and author have made every effort to trace and contact all copyright holders before publication. If notified, the publisher will be pleased to rectify any errors or omissions at the earliest opportunity.

Index

For the benefit of digital users, indexed terms that span two pages (e.g., 52–53) may, on occasion, appear on only one of those pages.

M

N

O

P

Q

DIPLOMACY
A Very Short Introduction
Joseph M. Siracusa

Like making war, diplomacy has been around a very long time, at least since the Bronze Age. It was primitive by today's standards, there were few rules, but it was a recognizable form of diplomacy. Since then, diplomacy has evolved greatly, coming to mean different things, to different persons, at different times, ranging from the elegant to the inelegant. Whatever one's definition, few could doubt that the course and consequences of the major events of modern international diplomacy have shaped and changed the global world in which we live. Joseph M. Siracusa introduces the subject of diplomacy from a historical perspective, providing examples from significant historical phases and episodes to illustrate the art of diplomacy in action.

'Professor Siracusa provides a lively introduction to diplomacy through the perspective of history.'

Gerry Woodard, Senior Fellow in Political Science at the University of Melbourne and former Australasian Ambassador in Asia

Science and Religion
A Very Short Introduction
Thomas Dixon

The debate between science and religion is never out of the news: emotions run high, fuelled by polemical bestsellers and, at the other end of the spectrum, high-profile campaigns to teach 'Intelligent Design' in schools. Yet there is much more to the debate than the clash of these extremes. As Thomas Dixon shows in this balanced and thought-provoking introduction, many have seen harmony rather than conflict between faith and science. He explores not only the key philosophical questions that underlie the debate, but also the social, political, and ethical contexts that have made 'science and religion' such a fraught and interesting topic in the modern world, offering perspectives from non-Christian religions and examples from across the physical, biological, and social sciences.

'A rich introductory text . . . on the study of relations of science and religion.'

R. P. Whaite, Metascience